# Nigeria's Foreign Policy Since 1999

Adonis & Abbey Publishers Ltd
Office: United Kingdom
85 Great Portland Street
First Floor
London W1W 7LT
Tel: 0845 873 0262
Website: http://www.adonis-abbey.com
E-mail Address: editor@adonis-abbey.com

Nigeria:
Plot 2560, Hassan Musa Katsina Street, Asokoro, Abuja, Nigeria
Tel: +234 (0) 7058078841/08052035034
Website: http://www.adonis-abbey.com
E-mail Address: editor@adonis-abbey.com

British Library Cataloguing-in-Publication Data
A catalogue record for this book is available from the British Library

ISBN: 9781913976279

# Nigeria's Foreign Policy Since 1999

George Awele Nwalie and Yao Nikez Adu

ADONIS & ABBEY
PUBLISHERS LTD

"In this book, George A. Nwalie and Yao N. Adu, provide an in-depth analysis of Nigeria's foreign policy since 1999, highlighting the implementation of Afrocentrism in Nigeria's foreign policy. It is a useful guide for foreign policy makers."

— Claire A Amuhaya (PhD), Senior Lecturer, Department of Theory and History of International Relations RUDN University Moscow, Russia

"The book, Nigeria's Foreign Policy Since 1999" by George A. Nwalie and Yao N. Adu, provides a timely analysis of foreign policy of one of the leading African states. The authors explore the centrist position of Nigeria in the formation of the Organization of African Unity, the Economic Community of West African States, the Niger River Basin Commission, the Lake Chad Basin Commission, the Gulf of Guinea Commission, and as well as its impacts on the international community and the core issues in Nigerian foreign policy and challenges facing the country.

— Nigusie Kassaye W. Michael, Dr. of Historical Sciences, Professor, Department of Theory and History of International Relations RUDN University Moscow, Russia

"The book, Nigeria's Foreign Policy Since 1999" by George A. Nwalie and Yao N. Adu, will be of great importance to the African continent, most especially the West African region as it will enable them to have access to several measures to tackle and implement foreign policy across the globe. The book is a useful addition to African History, African International Relations, African Politics, Foreign Policy Analysis, International Relations, and Regional Integration courses, as well as a tool for policy makers, diplomats, and the NGO community."

— Professor Konstantin A. Pantserev, Full-time Professor of the Department of Theory and History of International Relations, School of International Relations, Saint-Petersburg State University, Russia. E-mail: pantserev@yandex.ru

"The book, Nigeria's Foreign Policy Since 1999 by George A. Nwalie and Yao N. Adu, makes far-reaching suggestions on how to improve Nigeria's foreign policy to serve the national interest in the African continent and beyond. Thus, an in-depth analysis of Nigeria's relations with major powers makes this book a must-read."

—Professor Mamadou Keita,
Full-time Professor of Law Faculties,
Head of Public Law Faculty,
Faculty of Public Law and Political Sciences Bamako, Mali.Email: madouketa@yahoo.fr

# Table of Contents

Acronyms ..................................................................................................... ix

**Chapter One: Introduction** ..................................................................... 11
*1.1 Introduction* .......................................................................................... 11
*1.2 Conceptual and Historical Basis of Nigeria's Foreign Policy* ................. 15
*1.3 Historical Basis of Nigeria's Foreign Policy* .......................................... 17
*1.4 Nigeria's Foreign Policy in the Second and Third Republic* ................... 22
*1.5 Legal Basis of Nigeria's Foreign Policy* ................................................ 30
*1.6 Institutional Basis of Nigeria's Foreign Policy* ..................................... 32
*1.7 Afrocentrism in Nigeria's Foreign Policy* .............................................. 42

**Chapter 2: The Dynamics of Nigeria's Foreign Policy** ...................... 47
*2.1 Nigeria's Foreign Policy in Africa* ........................................................ 47
*2.2 Nigeria in AU* ...................................................................................... 49
*2.3 Nigeria and Her Contiguous Neighbours* .............................................. 66
*2.4 Nigeria and Multilateral Institutions in West Africa* ............................. 81

**Chapter 3: Nigeria's Relations with Major Powers** ........................... 109
*3.1 Nigeria-UK Relations* ......................................................................... 109
*3.2 Nigeria-USA Relations* ....................................................................... 117
*3.3 Nigeria-China Relations* ..................................................................... 122
*3.4 Nigeria-Russia Relations* .................................................................... 127
*3.5 Nigeria-France Relations* .................................................................... 131

**Chapter 4: Nigeria and the International Community** ....................... 137
*4.1 Nigeria and the United Nations* .......................................................... 137
*4.2 Nigeria-EU Relations* ......................................................................... 153
*4.3 Nigeria and the Commonwealth* ......................................................... 156

**Concluding Remarks** .............................................................................. 158
*Glossary* .................................................................................................... 167
*Bibliography* .............................................................................................. 177
*Index* ......................................................................................................... 195

## Acronyms

AfCFTA – African Continental Free Trade Agreement
APRM – Africa Peer Review Mechanism
AU – African Union
BIT – Bilateral Investment Treaty
BTT – Bilateral Taxation Treaty
BRICS – Brazil, Russia, India, China, and South Africa
CAF – Confederation of African Football
ECCAS – Economic Community of Central African States
CBAAC – Centre for Black African Arts and Civilisation
CLE- Council of Legal Education
CRESMAC – Regional Maritime Security of Central Africa
CRESMAO – Regional Centre for Maritime Security of West Africa
DICON – Defence Industries Corporation of Nigeria
DPR – Department of Petroleum Resources
ECCAS – Economic Community of Central African States
ECOMOG – ECOWAS Monitoring Group
ECOWAS – Economic Community of West African States
EEC – European Economic Community
EDF – European Development Fund
EMCP – ECOWAS Monetary Co-operation Programme
EU – European Union
FAO – Food and Agriculture Organisation
FDI – Foreign Direct Investment
FIFA – Federation of International Football Association
FMARD – Federal Ministry of Agriculture and Rural Development
FMWASD – Federal Ministry of Women Affairs and Social Development
FMYSD – Federal Ministry of Youth and Sports Development
FESTAC – African Festival Arts and Culture
FNLA – National Front for the Liberation of Angola
GGC – Gulf of Guinea Commission
HLP – High-Level-Panel
ICAO – International Civil Aviation Organisation
ILO – International Labour Organisation
IMF – International Monetary Fund
IMO – International Maritime Organisation

IOC – International Olympic Committee
LCBC – Lake Chad Basin Commission
MDA– Ministries Departments and Agencies
MFA– Ministry of Foreign Affairs
MDGs – Millennium Development Goals
MPLA –People's Movement for the Liberation of Angola
NAPTIP –National Agency for the Prohibition of Trafficking in Persons
NBA– Niger Basin Authority
NBC – National Boundary Commission
NDLEA– National Drug Law Enforcement Agency
NEPAD – New Partnership for Africa's Development
NIIA – Nigerian Institute of International Affairs
NNPC–Nigerian National Petroleum Corporation
NPFL – National Patriotic Front Rebel Army
OAU– Organisation of African Unity
OPEC – Organization of Petroleum Exporting Countries
PACIR– Presidential Advisory Council on International Relations
PTDF – Petroleum Technology Development Fund
SCO – Shanghai Cooperation Organisation
SAP – Structural Adjustment Program
SDGs – Sustainable Development Goals
SMS – Standing Mediation Committee
UN – United Nations
UNO – United Nations Organisation
UNESCO – United Nations Educational, Scientific and Cultural Organisation
UNGA – United Nations General Assembly
USA – United States of America
USSR – Union of Soviet Socialist Republic
WAFU – West African Football Union

# Chapter One

## Introduction

### 1.1 Introduction

The general optimism around the promise of consolidating Afrocentrism in Nigeria's foreign policy revolves around its economic power in Africa as well as the conceptual and ideological underpinnings of its foreign policy concept, which is centred on the pursuit, preservation, and protection of Africa's interests. Thus, the evolution of the concept of Nigeria's foreign policy in the contemporary period has made it possible to trace the process of changing its priorities in relations with African countries in the context of the regional and international situation.

As Machiavelli famously remarked, "The practice of diplomacy is essential for the state to maintain power and build reputation on an international level; thus, the opportunities for the state to form positive relations with foreign states are limited to certain situations"[1]. In the context of this statement, successive Nigerian presidents have shown much commitment towards promoting African diplomacy as well as representing the good image of Africans in the international community. Thus, the historical basis of Nigeria's foreign policy can be traced to 1960, which could be attributed to the Oliver Lyttleton Constitution of 1954, the John Macpherson Constitution of 1951, the Arthur Richards Constitution of 1946, and the Hugh Clifford Constitution of 1922. The constitutions laid the foundation upon which Nigeria's foreign policy was formulated. In general, there are three major institutions that are responsible for the formulation and implementation of Nigeria's foreign policy: the Ministry of Foreign Affairs (MFA), the Presidential Advisory Council on International Relations (PACIR), and the Nigerian Institute of International Affairs. Since Nigeria gained independence in 1960, the goals of its foreign policy institutions have been channelled towards the development of Africa. Moreover, the Afrocentric nature of Nigeria's foreign policy has

---

[1] Machiavelli, Niccolo. *The Prince and the Discourses.* New York: Modern Library, 1950.

made it absolutely inevitable for Nigeria to prioritise Africa in the interests of continental unity and complete decolonisation of the continent.

Since political independence, Nigeria has consistently shown commitment to promoting African diplomacy, acting as a defender of the interests of the "black diaspora" on a global scale, and defending the positive image of Africans in the international community. The concept of 'Africa as the centrepiece of Nigeria's foreign policy' was aimed at actualising its national interest and foreign policy objectives towards Africa'. Moreover, Nigeria's national interests were designed and structured by lovers of Pan-Africanism, who strongly believe in African unity and the solidarity of black people all over the world. As an active member of the African Union, Nigeria has continued to play a vital role in the socioeconomic initiatives of the Union.

Nigeria's participation in the formation of the Organisation of African Unity (OAU) and its transmutation to the African Union in 2002 are associated with the Afrocentric vector of its foreign policy. Nigeria took an active part in the struggle for decolonisation in Angola, Mozambique, Namibia, and the fight against apartheid in South Africa. In the context of cultural diplomacy, the Nigerian film industry has become the most effective tool of soft power to convey the cultural narrative of the country and has also acted as a tool to promote cultural diplomacy in Africa. Another aspect of Nigerian relations in Africa was based on the principles of partnership. Nigeria considers itself the natural leader of black Africa. But many African states, especially South Africa, are now openly challenging Nigeria's claims to the role of leader. In turn, French-speaking African states continue to rely on France in matters of internal and external security. In addition, the African direction of Nigeria's foreign policy in the twenty-first century contributed to solving complex problems in the system of modern public administration, which served as the basis for the economic recovery of African countries. Nigeria's participation in the economic initiatives of the New Partnership for Africa's Development (NEPAD) and the Agenda of the African Union for the period up to 2063 contributed to the deepening of economic cooperation with the states of the continent.

Chapter One  |  George Awele Nwalie and Yao Nikez Adu

12

Moreover, Nigeria has intensified efforts to establish and develop friendly relations with its neighbours, namely Benin, Niger, Chad, and Cameroon, as well as with other countries in the West African subregion. The guiding principles of Nigeria's regional foreign policy were the principles of good neighbourliness and friendship. As an active participant in the Niger River Basin Commission, the Lake Chad Basin Commission, and the Gulf of Guinea Commission, Nigeria not only maintained friendly relations with the member states of these international organisations, but also developed and implemented their development programmes. Nigeria was one of the founders of ECOWAS and has often initiated political and security decisions through this organisation, which are important for the entire region. The West African region has been an integral part of Nigeria's foreign policy. In the context of regional security, the Nigerian army is actively involved in ensuring peace under the leadership of responsible regional security organisations such as ECOWAS–ECOMOG.

However, the conception of regional integration provided an opportunity for Nigeria to exert its hegemonic influence in West Africa and beyond. It could be argued that Nigeria's leading role in ECOMOG was justified by the belief that no sacrifice was too great in the cause of peace and greater political and economic integration in the West African subregion.

However, Nigeria's relations with the major powers, the UK, USA, People's Republic of China, and the Russian Federation, are in the sectors of economy, security, culture, and education, to name a few. Following Nigerian relations with major powers, Nigeria-UK bilateral relations have been filled with multidimensional content in the political, diplomatic, defence, economic, and social spheres. The political and diplomatic dialogue between the two states is facilitated by their active cooperation through their membership in several international organisations. Meanwhile, Nigeria is currently the largest United States trading partner in sub-Saharan Africa, mainly due to the high export rate of Nigerian oil, which accounts for 8% of United States oil imports, which is half the daily oil production in Nigeria. While the Peoples Republic of China and Nigeria have been good partners in economic and trade relations, always trying to achieve mutual benefits and win-win outcomes. Furthermore, Nigeria's relationship with Russia began with the Union of Soviet Socialist Republics (USSR) and has lasted ever since. It is interesting to note that since 2019, after the first Russia-Africa Summit in Sochi, the Nigerian government has hosted several delegations from the Russian business community, taken part in many exhibitions, and is currently in a cordial relationship with the Russian Federation, mostly in the areas of trade and investment. Nonetheless, Nigeria, because of its demographic, economic, cultural, and political importance, has a crucial role in the international community.

Nigeria strives to maintain multilateral diplomatic relations through international organisations such as the United Nations. Nigeria participated in several peacekeeping missions, which earned it the international status of a partner in ensuring global stability and a leader in global peace and security. Nigeria is one of the leading African countries supporting the demand for a comprehensive reform of the UN. Moreover, Nigerian relations with the European Union became stronger in the early 2000s, essentially because of the Cotonou Partnership Agreement, which allows the EU to strengthen peace and security, economic, and regional integration, energy, and environmental sustainability in Africa. It became clear that the mutual relationship between Nigeria and EU member states (France and Germany) has been one of trade and security. French exports to Nigeria consist of refined petroleum products, pharmaceuticals, mechanical, electric, electronic, and computer equipment, and agro-food products, while exports from Nigeria to France are mainly made up of petroleum products. Meanwhile, Nigeria and Germany are actively involved in many bilateral relationships across broad-ranging sectors, including diplomacy, security, trade, and investment.

Thus, the monograph consists of the following four chapters: (1) Introduction; (2) Dynamics of Nigeria's Policy; (3) Nigeria's Relations with Major Powers; and (4) Nigeria and the International Community.

However, the monograph can be used as practical recommendations when considering relevant issues in ECOWAS, the Gulf of Guinea Commission, the Niger River Basin Authority, the Lake Chad Basin Commission, the African Union and the United Nations. Also, it can be used to develop lectures and read courses on the history of Africa's foreign policy, problems of international relations, and security in West Africa.

## 1.2 Conceptual and Historical Basis of Nigeria's Foreign Policy

The historical basis of Nigeria's foreign policy can be traced to the Oliver Lyttleton Constitution of 1954[2], the John Macpherson Constitution of 1951[3], the Arthur Richards Constitution of 1946,[4] and the Hugh Clifford Constitution of 1922[5] which arguably laid the foundation upon which Nigeria's foreign policy was formed. For instance, Item 18, Section II, Part I of The Implementation of Exclusive Legislative List, Nigerian Constitution Order in Council 1954 -1956[6] was a sessional document on foreign policy, which became the first foreign policy document of Nigeria. It is a product of the joint efforts of the Governor-General, his Chief Secretary, and the British Colonial and Commonwealth Reactions Offices[7]. Meanwhile, the Hugh Clifford Constitution of 1922, which replaced the abolished old legislative council for the Lagos colony and the Nigerian council, was believed to have initiated the foundation of Nigeria's foreign policy. The concept of Nigeria's foreign policy from inception is termed 'Afrocentrism.' At the initial stage, Nigeria's foreign policy objectives, which were devoted to Africa-oriented policies in the interest of continental unity and the total decolonization of the African continent,[8] witnessed a setback in its implementation because of the political will of Great Britain and the United States. Nigeria's foreign policy in the first republic was influenced by Her Majesty Queen Elizabeth II, Governor–General Sir James Wilson Robertson, and another Western element, which in turn limited the country's ability to pursue the pan–Africanism objectives adopted by the continent.

After a peaceful transition from the colonial period, Nigeria turned into an independent state that controlled its own affairs on both a domestic and international level. To communicate with the outside

---

[2] *The Oliver Lyttleton Constitution of 1954.*
[3] *The John Macpherson Constitution of 1951.*
[4] *The Arthur Richards Constitution of 1946.*
[5] *The Hugh Clifford Constitution of 1922.*
[6] *Nigerian Constitution Order in Council. 1954. with the Supplement to Official Gazette. 1960.*
[7] *Colonial Office of Great Britain: Report of the Resumed Conference on the Nigerian Constitution Came.1959. London: HMSG 1954.*
[8] *Official Gazette, Federal Republic of Nigeria 1999 Constitution (as amended) with the National Industrial Court. 98. (20). Government Notice No.103, The Federal Government Printer, Lagos, FGP 027/32011/2, 200 (OL13).*

Chapter One | George Awele Nwalie and Yao Nikez Adu

world, Nigeria has developed a complex of legal principles and goals for guiding such formal relationships. However, it has not always been so smooth since the foreign policy of Nigeria got over some ups and downs (Nwalie, 2020).

Since the independence of Nigeria in 1960, when Aja Nwachukwu was appointed as the first Minister of Foreign Affairs and Commonwealth Relations, later called just Foreign Affairs, the foreign policy of Nigeria has been oriented towards Africa as a regional power adhering to several crucial principles: unity and independence of all of Africa, the ability to exert influence in the region on the basis of hegemon rights, peaceful settlement of disputes and conflicts, non-interference in the internal affairs of other nations, as well as regional economic cooperation and development. In order to implement these principles, Nigeria is vigorously involved in the activities of the African Union, the Commonwealth of Nations, the Economic Community of West African States (ECOWAS), the Non-Aligned Movement, and the General Assembly of the United Nations.

The next key point details the national interests and goals of Nigeria's foreign policy.

- Nigeria's foreign policy metamorphosed from the colonial era to the post-independent period.
- It was in the post-independence era that a truly indigenous Nigeria's foreign policy emerged.
- By «truly indigenous Nigeria's foreign policy», we mean the dominance of foreign policymaking and implementation in Nigeria by Nigerians.
- In the post-independence period, Nigeria's foreign policy was not designed and directed to coincide with, nor to pursue, the interests of Her Majesty's government in England.
- Nigeria's foreign policy was anchored on certain principles that were designed to champion Nigerian causes.
- As stated by Aluko (1981), such principles were natural acts of respect for the sovereign equality of other nations, non-interference in the internal affairs of other nations, and engagement in collaboration as instruments of endorsing the unity of Africa.
- Such policy has remained the same, with some improvements to reflect local, global, political, and economic changes.

## 1.3 Historical Basis of Nigeria's Foreign Policy

Nigeria's foreign policy has been witnessing a drastic transformation since independence in 1960. On attaining independence, Nigeria became a bonafide member of the United Nations[9], Commonwealth, etc. The Lyttelton period is associated with the devolution of power for foreign affairs from Britain to the Federal Government of Nigeria (Eze, 2009).

However, when Nigeria attained self-governing status under the British government on 1 April 1957, Prime Minister Alhaji Tafawa Balewa personally took charge of the country's external relations portfolio. Meanwhile, the Ministry of Foreign Affairs and Commonwealth Relations was officially created in 1961, with Prime Minister Tafawa Balewa appointing Jaja Wachuku as the inaugural Minister of Foreign Affairs and Commonwealth Relations[10].

According to Fawole et al., (2003), Tafawa Balewa, during his early days as Prime Minister, retained the service of a Briton, Peter Stallard, as the secretary of the Nigerian government. Stallard was a de facto foreign affairs and Commonwealth Minister until 1961.

More importantly, after Nigeria was granted independence, Prime Minister Tafawa Balewa, in his inaugural speech on 7 October 1960, at the Plenary of the 15th Regular Session of the United Nations General Assembly, exactly six days after Nigeria gained independence and became the 99th member of the organisation, declared that Nigeria hoped to work with all African states for the progress of Africa and to assist in bringing all African territories to a state of responsible independence and help in finding a lasting solution to the problem affecting Nigeria's immediate neighbours[11].

---

[9] *The seventeen African countries that became members of UN during the year of Africa, are as follow: Benin, on September 20, 1960; Burkina Faso, on September 20, 1960; Cameroon, on September 20, 1960; Central African Republic, on September 20, 1960; Chad, on September 20, 1960; Congo, on September 20, 1960; Cote d'Ivoire, on September 20, 1960; Democratic Republic of the Congo, on September 20, 1960; Gabon, on September 20, 1960; Ghana, on March 8, 1957; Guinea, on December 17, 1958; Madagascar, on September 20, 1960; Mali, on September 28, 1960; Niger, on September 20, 1960; Nigeria, on October 1, 1960; Senegal, on September 28, 1960; Somalia, on September 20, 1960; Togo, on September 20, 1960; Mauritania, on October 27, 1961.*

[10]*Nigeria Ministry of Foreign Affairs. Great Nation, United in Diversity.*

[11]*Statement by Abubakar Tafawa Balewa. Prime Minister of the Federal Republic of Nigeria at the United Nations General Assembly, New York, October 7, 1960. Maiden General Assembly Statement at the United Nations.*

Furthermore, Nigeria's foreign policy concept is traced to the then Prime Minister Tafawa Balewa's administration, which instituted Nigeria's sovereign statehood and its dynamic foreign policy. The concept of dynamic foreign policy first penetrated the intellectual discourse on Nigeria's foreign policy in the first republic. This was on the occasion of the parliamentary debate on Nigeria's foreign policy; accordingly, the then Minister of Foreign Affairs, Jaja Anucha Wachuku, presented a proposal to the honourable house to confirm Nigeria's foreign policy. As proclaimed by the Prime Minister, it would be approved by the honorary chamber on 20 August 1960; thus, the house declared his approval of the interpretation and conduct of the government and congratulated the government on its achievements in the international community from the moment the country gained independence (Pine, 2011).

Accordingly, the then shadow foreign minister Anthony Enahoro amended the proposal to read: The Honourable Chamber considers that the foreign policy of the federal government is proclaimed by the Prime Minister and approved on August 20, 1960; this Honourable Chamber lacks dynamism and regrets that the interpretation and behaviour of the government are not consistent with the progressive opinion in Africa (Pine, 2011). In retort, the Foreign Affairs Minister Jaja Anucha Wachuku went on to reel out the foreign policy engagements of Nigeria and how these engagements were dynamic, saying that if these measures were not dynamic, then he does not know what dynamic constitutes[12].

Thus, the concept of dynamism has been the fundamental basis for developing and evaluating foreign policy in Nigeria. During the discussion, it was arduous to realise the concept of dynamism, its usefulness, and its importance in the foreign policy process. Relatively, the statement that aimed at conceptual operationalisation was the radical rhetoric of Anthony Enahoro that the lower groups in the country represent the authentic voice and the true nature of the people of the country and that, as such, any foreign policy measure beyond their sympathies is lacking in enthusiasm and not dynamic (Pine, 2011).

---

[12]*House of Representatives Debates on Federation of Nigeria, August 20, 1960, cols 2669 – 71.*

Meanwhile, the administrations of Abubakar Tafawa Balewa and Shehu Shagari were considered conservative, while the administration of Musa Yar'Adua was considered dynamic. Due to the public appeal of the denomination of radicalism and dynamism, it is politically unreliable for successive regimes from the time of independence in the first republic to mark their foreign policy as dynamic due to the Western world's influence.

However, it should be noted that the national interests of the nation, not the outpouring of dynamism or its absence, are a barometer for measuring its foreign policy. To buttress this, Nigeria pursued a dynamic foreign policy towards the United States of America while sustaining the fundamental principle of consistently having Africa as the focal point of its foreign policy (Abegunrin 2003). He believed Nigeria's foreign policy is deeply rooted in Africa, highlighting political and economic cooperation, peaceful dispute resolution, and global non-alignment, which sometimes conflict with the United States' foreign policies and national goals. However, under the first republic, the ineffectiveness of the dynamic foreign policy concept was caused by the laid-down structure and influence of the Western world[13].

Nevertheless, during this period of dynamism, Nigeria witnessed both civilian and military administrations with various approaches to executing their foreign policy objectives, as observed in the evolution of Nigeria's foreign policy from one administration to another since 1960 (Ebegbulem, 2019). Additionally, Nigeria's foreign policy has been guided by certain principles and objectives in the context of international relations, which include the protection of the country's national interest, among others, sovereignty and protection of territorial integrity, devotion to Africa-oriented policies in the interest of continental unity, and total decolonisation of the African continent (Akindele, 1990).

It is imperative to note that Nigeria's Afrocentric foreign policy has been in existence since the first republic. Article 19(b) of the 1979 Constitution of the Federal Republic of Nigeria encapsulates Nigeria's foreign policy objectives to include: (1) promotion of African

---

[13] *Colonial Office of Great Britain: Report of the Resumed Conference on the Nigerian Constitution Came.1959. London: HMSG 1954.*

integration and support of African unity; (2) promotion of international cooperation for the consolidation of universal peace and mutual respect among all nations; and (3) elimination of discrimination in all its manifestation[14]. Thus, the idea of Africa as a central part of Nigeria's foreign policy is based on the understanding that Nigeria's participation in the system of international relations will be examined through binoculars in Africa. Jaja Anucha Wachuku argued that Nigeria's foreign policy should be centred on Africa because charity begins at home (Pine, 2011).

The problems that practically expressed this African focus were the remnants of colonialism on the continent, Apartheid in South Africa, the liberation wars, and ideological and indirect conflicts (proxy wars), among others. It is crucial to note that the Nigerian representative at the 16th Special Session of the United Nations General Assembly in 1989 voted in favour of South Africa during the deliberation of Apartheid and its destructive consequences[15].

Moreover, outside of these politically urgent factors, the problem of a familiar racial universe, cultural neighbourhood, shared historical experience, and the ideals of Pan-Africanism have even more oiled the wheels of this conceptualisation of foreign policy. Indeed, pursuing an African-oriented foreign policy based on Africans' racial and socio-cultural affinity.

As part of Africa's centredness in Nigeria's foreign policy, Nigeria was immensely involved in the struggle for decolonisation in Angola, Mozambique, and Namibia. There was a struggle against Apartheid in South Africa, even though it was geographically far from the southern region of Africa. Nigeria is central to the formation of ECOWAS, restrains the destruction of public order in Liberia and Sierra Leone, and has contributed hugely to peacekeeping operations and providing economic incentives for less economically demanding African states (Saliu, 2012).

It is crucial to mention that Nigeria's Afrocentric foreign policy is consistently centred on uniting and promoting Africa's political, economic, and sociocultural activities, despite a few dissenting voices on its foreign policy decisions towards Africa. Nigeria's commitment

---

[14]*The Constitution of the Federal Republic of Nigeria 1979 // ConstitutionNet.*
[15]*United Nations General Assembly Declaration on South Africa. 1989.*

to the decolonisation of Africa and the right of Africans to self-determination validated this fact. For instance, Nigeria deployed its diplomatic prowess through global support, such as direct bilateral financial and material aid to the Liberation Movements across the continent.

In the context of cultural relations, Nollywood Nigeria's movie industry has emerged as the most effective soft-power instrument to transmit the country's cultural narrative to the outside world. It is also a tool for facilitating cultural diplomacy in Africa. Nollywood has overshadowed both Hollywood and Bollywood in Africa and is the essential source of movies on the continent (Global, 2012). The South African multinational cable television corporation, DStv, offers a dedicated Nollywood movie channel (African Magic) that transmits these movies across the continent with tens of millions of subscribers. Thus, Nollywood not only accrues an economic gain for Nigeria but also dispenses valuable entertainment and transmits Nigerian cultural values across the continent and beyond. Sledzevski (2019) examined the cultural and religious practices of the peoples of tropical Africa in the context of globalising the post-secular world. He argues that the role of Christianity and Islam in the cultural self-determination of the peoples of tropical Africa in the 20th–early 21st century has impacted African theological thought, which indirectly influences the religious component in the cultural identity of Africans relating to African foreign policy.

It is also of significance to note that Nigeria engaged in a vital role in the liberation of Guinea-Bissau, Mozambique, Rhodesia (now Zimbabwe), Sao Tome and Principe, Cape Verde, Angola, and South Africa (Gambari, 1997) Aluko (1976) views Nigeria's Afrocentric foreign policy as an instrument used in pursuing the objectives of pan-Africanism, which in turn leads to the unification of the continent.

However, Oshewolo (2019b) claimed that the Afrocentric foreign policy describes Nigeria's leadership status and role towards Africa. He believed that Nigeria's contributions have always brought a sense of entitlement to shaping the activities of international relations in Africa. According to Cyril

(2008), Afrocentric foreign policy primarily connects the pursuit of Nigeria's foreign policy to its quest for leadership on the continent. Thus, Afrocentric foreign policy facilitated Nigeria's ambitions towards gaining international recognition and helped harmonise the continent to achieve the Pan-African objectives.

Ultimately, Nigeria, in the first republic, used Afrocentric foreign policy as a tool to exemplify its leadership role in Africa and beyond[16]. Notably, it is indicated in such areas as the eradication of colonialism and white minority rule in countries such as Angola, Guinea-Bissau, Mozambique, Namibia, Zimbabwe, and South Africa, and its aid to countries like Angola, Benin, Botswana, Zambia, and Zimbabwe, and its peacekeeping in countries such as Liberia, Sierra Leone, and the Democratic Republic of Congo (Sandra, 2012).

## *1.4 Nigeria's Foreign Policy in the Second and Third Republics*

Nigeria's foreign policy in the Second Republic was observed during President Shehu Shagari's tenure. However, Shagari's tenure marked Nigeria's second attempt at democratic governance following the chain of events that began in January 1960 and culminated in the Nigeria–Biafra civil war of 1967-1970 (Nwalie, 2020), which saw Nigeria's first military regime from 1966-1979. However, President Shehu Shagari, in the second republic, inherited a foreign policy that was radical in its departure from Murtala Muhammed and Olusegun Obasanjo. Moreover, the foreign policy credentials of the Murtala Muhammed and Olusegun Obasanjo regimes were intimidating and radical. For the first time in history, Nigeria, despite the position of the United States and Britain, recognised the nationalist Popular Movement for the Liberation of Angola (MPLA) and donated a huge amount of money to the government, leading the party in Angola (Garba, 1987).

In this light, Shubin (2013) argued that the decision of the Union of Soviet Socialist Republics (USSR) in the Angola conflict was contrary to the position of some great power states, such as the United States and Great Britain. He claimed that the USSR engaged in a strategic alliance with the Popular Movement for the Liberation of Angola, contributing to the movement's success. He was of the opinion that the strategic alliance between the USSR and Angola helped to survive South Africa's military incursions in Angola from the National Union for the Total Independence of Angola in the early 1970s until the late 1980s

---

[16] *The Constitution of the Federal Republic of Nigeria 1979 // ConstitutionNet.*

Accordingly, the foreign policy objectives of the President Shagari administration, which aimed to promote African unity, suffered some setbacks because of Nigeria's economic fortune, which was depleted as a result of corruption, inflation, and Western influence (Nwalie, 2020). Western influence was the main obstacle to achieving Nigeria's foreign policy objectives under President Shehu Shagari's administration. Nigeria's foreign policy structure, which the Governor-General laid down during the colonial period, allowed Great Britain to interfere in Nigeria's foreign policy.

During the General Ibrahim Babangida administration, the concept of economic diplomacy was introduced into Nigeria's foreign policy. This was to facilitate export trade and investment and increase financial assistance from friendly states (Saliu, 1994).

In line with this judgement, Foreign Affairs Minister General Ike Nwachukwu, in his speech at the National Assembly entitled "The Dynamics of Foreign Policy of Nigeria," reiterated the direction of Nigeria's foreign policy implementation in Africa. He declared that Nigeria's foreign policy is the apparatus responsible for promoting the national economic recovery programme (Saliu, 1994). For instance, in 1975, at the peak of Nigeria's economic recovery following a devastating civil war, Nigeria nudged other subregional countries to establish ECOWAS (Saliu, 1994).

The Babangida administration adopted economic diplomacy as a foreign policy instrument in a bid to tackle Nigeria's financial challenges through the Structural Adjustment Programme (SAP) and subsequently to re-energised Nigeria's hegemony in Africa, as documented by Imuokhede (2016). Chidozie (2014) argued that the Structural Adjustment Programme (SAP) experienced during the Babangida regime was due to the widespread corruption within the country. He asserted the annulment of the June 12, 1993, presidential election to usher in a democratically elected government. Instead, he created a contraption tagged as an interim government, which General Sani Abacha later overthrew in a palace coup. The constraints placed on the foreign policy framework concerning the topic of economic diplomacy were brought about by the financial strain Nigeria's economy was under as a result of the implementation of the so-called Structural Adjustment Programme (SAP). The most incredible attention was on the promotion of exports, debt restructuring, foreign direct investments, the adoption of neoliberal economic measures, and deep participation in the interaction of the international economy. The political aspect of the economic diplomacy programme was that Nigeria would revive and develop the goodwill and friendship of the leading countries in the world. Nevertheless, the main problem with SAP was Nigeria's inability to achieve economic benefits from its foreign policy ventures, especially in the subregion.

To reinforce this, Saliu (1994) insisted that the thrust of this policy was to make Nigeria's foreign policy serve the purpose of economic development at home, given that the regime inherited a prostrate economy from its predecessors. He believed that Nigeria could only survive the situation by seeking and securing the goodwill and support of friendly nations that have had a long history of good relations with Nigeria. However, the economic reforms under the Babangida administration were compelled to correct the economic downturn experienced during the period of military interregnum, which its administration inherited, as well as rekindle Nigeria's relationship with friendly countries[17].

**Redeeming Nigeria's Image in the Fourth Republic.** The emergence of Olusegun Obasanjo as Executive President of Nigeria in 1999 paved the way for the fourth republic. The key priority of Nigeria's foreign policy since the Fourth Republic is to redeem the image destroyed during the military regime[18]. To achieve the set objectives, Foreign Affairs Minister Sule Lamido introduced the following concepts of Nigeria's foreign policy: citizen diplomacy and economic diplomacy (Ajaebili et al., 2011).

In light of this, Obasanjo's administration engaged in shuttle diplomacy to restore the image of Nigeria the past administration destroyed and promote cordial relations with all nations, especially the African states. According to Sanubi et al. (2017), shuttle diplomacy is another way of improving Nigeria's multilateral relations in the international community. He believed that if fully implemented, it would help to correct the image of Nigerians in the outside world.

---

[17]*Nigeria. Structural Adjustment Program: Policies, Implementation, and Impact // The World Bank. 1994.*
[18]*Inaugural Speech of President Olusegun Obasanjo, 29 May, 1999, Federal Ministry of Information, Abuja*

Chapter One | George Awele Nwalie and Yao Nikez Adu

However, President Olusegun's administration introduced shuttle diplomacy to rekindle bilateral Nigerian-African relations and reposition Nigeria as the giant of Africa before the international community[19].

The Obasanjo administration was interested in the involvement of Nigerians, both home and abroad, in the activities of governance and national development. In line with his judgement, his contributions to national development served as a medium through which the people's living standards were improved[20].

Although the concept of citizen diplomacy appears self-explanatory, it is not precisely so; nevertheless, in the context of diplomacy as a political concept, Ozoemenam (2007) viewed citizen diplomacy as a constructive and well-organised action taken by the Nigerian government to achieve the objectives set by policymakers. Okocha et al. (2007) argued that citizen diplomacy is tailored towards protecting the image and integrity of Nigerian citizens both home and abroad and retaliating against countries that are hostile and who brand Nigeria as a corrupt nation.

While Akinterinwa (2007) explains further that, as conceptualised individuals, Nigerians are to be the primary focus of any foreign policy endeavour, in other words, they are to be made principal stakeholders and first beneficiaries of Nigeria's foreign policy efforts in any of Nigeria's foreign policy concentric circles. Importantly, they are to be specially empowered to respond to the changing challenges of globalisation wherever they may be found.

Also, Ogunsanwo (2007) asserts that citizen diplomacy could mean that, from the inception of the policy, Nigerian citizens abroad would become the central element of Nigeria's national interest. Thus, the country's unimpaired diplomatic machinery should be intended to protect its interests and economic welfare. He further indicated that any diplomacy that does not take this into consideration would not be annexed for diplomatic missions abroad.

Meanwhile, Abati (2009) documented that the Nigerian government does not appraise the lives of its citizens regarding the

---

[19]*Inaugural Speech of President Olusegun Obasanjo, 29 May 1999, Federal Ministry of Information, Abuja.*
[20]*Report of Activities of President Olusegun Obasanjo, Understanding Obasanjo's leadership and lesson // The Nations. January 20, 2013.*

dividend of democracy. Nigerians have been attacked in South –Africa; others were brutalised in Asia routinely, and some were even beheaded in Saudi Arabia. At home and in the Diaspora, Nigerians are left to their own survival tactics. They have learned not to expect anything from their government. Accordingly, the citizen diplomacy concept introduced in Obasanjo's administration reassured the citizenry of the inclusiveness in the foreign policy decision–making process[21].

However, after the end of the Olusegun Obasanjo administration, citizen diplomacy appears not to have yielded the envisaged dividend due to some factors that are both domestic and international. Considering the citizen to be at the centre of the national programme reinforces the original purpose of the government. When those in power provide the necessary leadership, they will, without much effort, secure the trust of the general populace and create centres of national solidarity and more agents for national progress. It is imperative to mention that the Olusegun Obasanjo administration reintroduced the economic diplomacy concept to reform and rebuild a more robust economy in Nigeria. However, this concept involves the policy-making, decision-making, and advocating of the sending countries' business interests and requires the application of technical expertise that analyses the effects of the countries (receiving countries) economic situation on their political climate and the sending countries' economic interests. In line with this judgement, President Olusegun Obasanjo claimed that economic diplomacy is a guide to improving Nigerian-African economic growth. He believed that the reform encourages the private sector, diversifies the economy, and delivers forward-thinking leadership for the continent of Africa[22].

Accordingly, the concept's scope comprises domestic and international economic matters, including the rule of economic relations between countries. The increased globalisation and the resultant interdependence among countries have pushed economic diplomacy to go deeper into domestic decision-making to cover policies relating to the production and exchange of goods and

---

[21] *Inaugural Speech of President Olusegun Obasanjo, 29 May, 1999, Federal Ministry of Information, Abuja.*
[22] *An interview with Olusegun Obasanjo: Up close and a little too personal // African Argument. September 28, 2017.*

services. However, economic diplomacy was designed to encourage and promote investment from inception to the signing of contracts and even market the business activities of the entire nation. The concept encourages diplomats to conduct trade and seminars, attend trade shows, visit potential investors, and be proactive in marketing the country. As a result, the concept under the Obasanjo administration increased the economic growth and development of Nigeria. Finally, Olusegun Obasanjo's foreign policy implementations during his military regime as Head of State from 1976 to 1979 and later as President in a democratic regime from 1999 to 2007 were considered to be different. For instance, Nigeria's foreign policy under the Olusegun Obasanjo military regime was a radical departure due to its attributes in Nigeria's military decrees [1]. At the same time, the latter was conservative because of its rationale. This revolved around restoring Nigeria's image, which was destroyed during the military regime. However, Olusegun Obasanjo, as Nigeria's second executive president, added more value to Nigeria's foreign policy due to the determining factors associated with the concept of Nigeria's foreign policy.

President Umaru Musa Yar'Adua's administration (2007 – 2010)[23] is not excluded, as he introduced the seven-point agenda in order to enhance the Nigerian economy and the living standards of the people. The Yar'Adua administration centred its foreign policy on Nigerian citizens and how to protect and ameliorate the living conditions of Nigerians. Ikedinachi et al. (2015) posited that the citizen diplomacy concept under the President Umaru Musa Yar'Adua administration has minimal impact on Nigerian citizens in spite of the approach and its level of acceptance by the public. In Gbadebo's (2018) opinion, President Yar'Adua's concept of citizen diplomacy was channelled to internal affairs. According to him, the president believed that the dilapidated infrastructure that could not be developed was more crucial to Nigeria and its citizens than the issue of the traditional foreign policy of Afrocentrism. Pantserev (2010) describes obstacles that revolve around information policy under Yar'Adua's administration and hinder Nigeria's participation in international programmes.

---

[23] *Seven Point Agenda of the Federal Republic of Nigeria. Nigeria High Commission // Nigerian Ministry of Foreign Affairs, Abuja, Aso Rock. 2010.*

Furthermore, President Musa Yar's Adua approaches to implementing citizen diplomacy affected Nigeria's commitment to international politics. During the later days of Musa Yar' Adua's administration, the Nigerian senate adopted a new doctrine called the "doctrine of necessity," which enabled the vice president to fill the vacuum that was created because of Musa Yar' Adua's inability to hand over power before his death in 2010[24].

After he won the presidential election in 2011, President Goodluck Jonathan brought a new idea called the transformation agenda into the political landscape to reconcile that which had affected bilateral relations between Nigeria and Africa. The transformation agenda introduced was designed to revive every decaying sector in the country. However, the transformation agenda is also passive and is considered citizen diplomacy. However, it was argued that the new agenda failed to accomplish its purpose because of the high level of insecurity, the Boko Haram activities in Northeast Nigeria, and corruption in government offices (Mantzikos, 2010; Walter, 2013).

Subsequently, the foreign policy of President Jonathan's administration revolves around domestic agendas. President Jonathan's foreign policy priority was investment and economic cooperation, which, according to him, were paramount to the country's national interest[25].

In the same light, Adeola (2015) claimed that President Jonathan maintained, to a large extent, President Yar'Adua's foreign policy goals but adopted the instruments of shuttle and economic diplomacy in rebranding Nigeria's image in a bid to attract foreign investments. However, citizen diplomacy was projected to improve citizen welfare and national image-building. In addition, the citizen diplomacy under President Jonathan's administration was objectively channelled to consolidate good governance, both home and abroad, as well as revive every decaying sector in the country.

After Muhammadu Buhari was sworn in as President of the Federal Republic of Nigeria in 2015, he introduced three key agendas

---

[24]*Doctrine of Necessity // Sahara Reporter, Feb 13, 2010.*
[25]*President Goodluck Jonathan. A Bad Account of an Equally Inglorious Era //the Nations. November 26, 2018.*

to tackle insecurity, economic instability, and corruption[26], aimed at restoring Nigeria's core value and glory in the community of nations.

However, President Buhari's new agendas were not a deviation from the previous foreign policy concept but were initiated by the government to address the prevailing domestic situation in Nigeria. President Buhari's administration saw issues confronting the country, such as the activities of Boko Haram insurgents, the ailing economy, and corruption inherited from the previous government, as a thrust caused by a specific element within the country[27]. However, the president believes that diversification of the country's economy can revive and attract foreign investors to the country.

Meanwhile, the Buhari administration opined that effective and dynamic foreign policy required a solid and functional domestic base in a prosperous Nigerian state[28]. Odubajo (2017) documented that the foreign policy agenda of President Buhari's administration is targeted at courting regional cooperation, attracting foreign direct investments (FDIs), and partnering with states, especially Western nations, in the fight against corruption. President Buhari's administration, similar to its predecessors, adopted economic diplomacy as a foreign policy tool. Given this scenario, it becomes imperative to enforce his economic revival strategy, which, to a large extent, has attracted foreign investment despite the attacks of the Boke Haram insurgency in the northern part of the country.

Finally, the foreign policy postures of Buhari's administration have been mainly concerned with and tasked with various reforms in bilateral trade, investment, security, and anti-corruption-oriented domestic and foreign policies. However, it is significant to note that its administration has been immensely criticised for misdirecting political will and resources. These criticisms have led to various arguments about the appropriateness of the administration's foreign policy strategies, the length of their successes, and the sustainability of their actions in promoting and improving Nigeria's image at home and abroad.

---

[26]*Inaugural Speech of President Muhammadu Buhari on 29 May 2015, Permanent Mission of Nigeria to the United Nations.*
[27] *NTA @GMN, Abuja, Nigeria, 4 February. 2019.*
[28]*Speech Delivered at the Maiden Interactive Session with the Diplomatic Corps Held at Rotunda Hall, Ministry of Foreign Affairs, Abuja on 12 December. 2015.*

## *1.5 Legal Basis of Nigeria's Foreign Policy*

Section 19 of the Nigerian Constitution of 1999 contains the objectives of Nigeria's foreign policy. According to the section, Nigerian foreign policy objectives should be as follows:

- Promotion and protection of national interests;
- Promoting African integration and supporting African unity;
- Promoting international collaboration in order to consolidate world peace and mutual respect between all peoples and eliminate discrimination in all its manifestations;
- Respect for international law and contractual obligations, as well as the desire to resolve international disputes through negotiation, arbitration, conciliation, and judicial decision, and also by promoting a fair global economic order.[29]

More importantly, the Nigeria's fundamental foreign policy principles and objectives have remained unchanged since independence. However, every succeeding administration in the country has adopted new mechanisms tailored towards the achievement of its foreign policy goal. The primary responsibility of all foreign policymakers is to articulate in clear terms their country's national interests and relate them to those of other nations within the international system. Nevertheless, the achievement of foreign policy goals presupposes the existence of reliable and universally recognised general principles on which a common foreign policy is based (Dauda, 2006).

Dauda (2006) noted that it is important to stress the fact that irrespective of the changes in government, the principles and objectives of Nigeria's foreign policy, as laid down by the late Prime Minister, Balewa, have remained basically the same. What was noticeable in all the continuities and discontinuities was in the area of emphasis. The principles which have upheld Nigeria's foreign policy since independence include the following: protection of the sovereignty and territorial integrity of the Nigerian State, promotion of the socio-economic well-being of Nigeria, enhancing Nigeria's image and status in the world at large, respect for the sovereignty and

---

[29]*Landmark University. Constitutional Basis of Nigerian Foreign Policy.*

territorial integrity of other states, non-interference in the internal affairs of other states, promotion of the unity and solidarity of African States, total political, economic, social, and cultural emancipation and rejuvenation of Africa, an unflinching commitment to the liberation of countries still under colonial rule, as well as removal of remaining vestiges of colonialism in Africa (UN, 1991)[30] .

Africa remains the centre of Nigeria's foreign policy. Nigeria's main challenges in Africa were promoting peace, prosperity, stability, and development in Africa, promoting political goodwill and understanding between African countries, despite the cultural, linguistic, and economic barriers raised by colonialism. Countering international intervention and presence in Africa and promoting the rapid socio-economic development of Africa through regional economic integration, strengthening subregional economic institutions and reducing economic dependence on extracontinental powers, the development of cultural cooperation as a means of strengthening political relations with all African countries, and finally, self-determination for all counties on the continent, the elimination of apartheid in South Africa, and the elimination of all forms of racial discrimination in Africa (UN, 1991).

Until now, Nigeria's foreign policy has concentrated on Africa. It considers itself the natural leader of black Africa. But many African states, particularly South Africa, now openly challenge Nigeria's claim to being the leader of Africa. The francophone African states also continue to rely on France for their internal and external security. Nigeria is now in search of a new role in Africa and in international affairs. This situation is an indication that Nigeria's capabilities has greatly diminished over the years. For instance, Nigeria has the second-largest army by number of troops on the continent, but due to political instability and a lack of equipment, it has been ranked just the 4th strongest country in Africa, according to (Global Firepower Ranking, 2016).

Even though Nigeria started well at independence by maintaining a decent consistency in making Africa the centrepiece of its foreign policy, a lot of internal political and economic problems, especially the military interregnums, oil boom, and excessive external interference in

---

[30] *United Nations Report, 1991*

its domestic affairs, have waned its influence and respect in the international community. This has led many people to brand Nigeria as a sleeping giant. However, such crucial factors as endemic corruption and unpatriotic regimes were drastically slowing down the development over the years, making it snail-paced. This has led to an image problem for Nigeria in the international political arena, which was profoundly evident in a statement by former British Prime Minister David Cameron describing Nigeria as «"fantastically corrupt"»[31].

## *1.6 Institutional Basis of Nigeria's Foreign Policy*

It is generally believed that Nigerian foreign policy objectives and national interests centred on Africa make it highly inevitable for its institutional system to contribute hugely to African foreign policy. It has become an established norm for independent and sovereign nations to engage in external relations. In other words, gaining independence by a state confers on that state the sovereign power to conduct foreign policy, which is seen in all independent countries of the world. For instance, Nigeria started its foreign policy in 1960 (the year it gained independence from Britain) under the late Abubakar Tafawa Balewa[32].

Before 1960, the country had no independent foreign policy since Lagos was still a colony, while the Northern, Eastern, and Western regions were Protectorates of Great Britain that controlled its external relations[33]. Thus, since independence and with the establishment of the ministry of external relations, the Nigerian government has continued to engage in foreign relations and the making of foreign policy. The Presidency and the National Assembly are two crucial actors whose roles are spelled out in the Constitution. As stated in the Constitution, the Presidency is in charge of the day-to-day responsibility for making policies, both domestic and foreign, while the National Assembly is empowered to make laws for governing the country in line with the

---

[31] Statement by the UK's Prime Minister, David Cameron, Nigeria is fantastically corrupt // Vanguard, May 10, 2016.
[32]*Nigeria Ministry of Foreign Affairs. Great Nation, United in Diversity.*
[33]*Nigerian Constitution Order in Council. 1954. with the Supplement to Official Gazette. 1960. Part D. 47 (20).*

---

country's domestic and external affairs. Moreover, the Ministry of Foreign Affairs is also charged with managing the country's external affairs.

Since the independence of Nigeria in 1960, Jaja Anucha Wachuku has been the first substantive Nigerian Minister of Foreign Affairs and Commonwealth Relations, later called External Affairs. Nigeria's foreign policy has been Africa-oriented with several fundamental principles, such as unity and independence for all of Africa, the ability to exert influence in the region based on hegemon rights, peaceful settlement of disputes and conflicts, noninterference in the internal affairs of other nations, and regional economic cooperation and development. To implement these principles, Nigeria is vigorously involved in the work of the African Union, the Commonwealth of Nations, the Economic Community of West African States (ECOWAS), the Non-Aligned Movement, and the United Nations. Lobashova (2021), while examining the foreign policy activity of Nigeria at the present stage, claims that the relationship between Nigeria and African countries is based on five existing principles of foreign policy, which are highlighted above. She argues that Nigeria must resolve its internal problems to implement its foreign policy goals in Africa effectively.

It is imperative to note that the Nigeria National Assembly (Upper Chamber) and the Nigeria House of Representatives (Lower Chamber), also known as the Senate and the House of Representatives, respectively, are the only statutory organs that can raise a motion on the floors of their respective houses and ratify any issue of foreign relations[34]. For emphasis, the Lower chamber makes laws and scrutinises the work of the executive arm of government, while the upper chamber considers bills approved by the lower chamber and further enacts them into law. Nevertheless, both chambers together constitute the Parliament.

Again, the National Assembly has the authority to tame international treaties and agreements signed by the country. Chapter I, Section 12 of the 1999 Constitution states that no treaty between the Federation and another country has the force of law, except to the

---

[34] *Federation of Nigeria. House of Representatives Debates. September 4, 1961. Col. 281.; House of Representatives Debates on Federation of Nigeria, August 20, 1960, cols 2669 – 71.*

extent that the National Assembly has enacted any such treaty. It is understood that no treaties or covenants signed or ratified in international forums, summits, or meetings can enter into force unless the National Assembly enact them. The National Assembly decides which treaties or covenants should be tamed.

For instance, military intervention, treaty ratification, and other foreign policy-related issues can only be implemented by the executive arm of government, which is also known as the presidency, after the consent and approval of the National Assembly, Chapter 1, Part 12 of the 1999 Constitution, entitled 'Powers of the Federal Republic of Nigeria.

Interestingly, the Presidency is the primary institution built around the office of the President of the Federal Republic of Nigeria to assist him in his day-to-day obligations. Since independence, its name has changed from the office of the Cabinet of Ministers, as it was previously known during the First Republic, to the Presidential Administration in the Second Republic and its current nomenclature, the Presidency. Throughout the world, the President is central to the state's foreign diplomacy, although some mechanisms and structures force the President and Presidency to adapt to internal pressure and constraints in foreign policy (Akinyemi, 2009).

According to Fawole (2003), the executive power embodied by the president is very powerful in executing and enforcing the law. The President directs and enforces the nation's affairs, including domestic and foreign affairs. The President's executive-legislative list functions include conducting foreign affairs, holding top-level diplomacy, negotiating and signing bilateral and multilateral treaties and agreements, receiving ambassadors and high commissioners, and attending meetings.

Despite the President being the commander in chief of the armed forces, he cannot allocate the country's military resources for peace or war without the consent of the Senate. Section 2 of the 1999 Constitution, entitled Powers of the Federal Republic of Nigeria, stated in Article 4(a) that the President should not declare a state of war between the Federation and another country unless with the permission of both sides of the House (National Assembly and House of Representatives) joint meeting[35]. Article 5 of the same section also states that the President, in agreement with the National Defense Council, may send Federation troops to limited military service outside of Nigeria if he is convinced that national security is in imminent danger.

Provided that the President, within seven days after the actual combat, must have requested the consent of the Senate, the Senate must give or refuse the specified consent within fourteen days (Constitution of the Federal Republic, 1999)[36]. The President is also authorised to negotiate and implement treaties on matters included in the exclusive list. However, the Constitution states that such treaties must be adopted and approved by the National Assembly (Upper and Lower Chambers) before they are considered law.

Despite the limitations of the President's authority, according to the provisions of the Constitution, the President remains the highest authority and determining factor in the development of the country's policy. The President can send bills or treaties to the National Assembly to enact into law, though the National Assembly may decide to agree or not. However, the President can still reject signing the bills adopted by the National Assembly (Nwalie et al., 2022).

For instance, the administration of President Muhammadu Buhari rejected signing into law the budget adopted by the National Assembly in 2018. He argued that the budget was full of contradictions and accused the legislature of falsifying the budget sent to them. However, this resulted in the delay of the signing of the budget into law by the president[37].

Accordingly, Nigeria's foreign policy objectives centred on African affairs made it highly inevitable for all the institutional systems responsible for their foreign policy obligations to always consider the interests of the African continent in their decision-making process. The Nigerian institutions, such as executive and legislative arms, are not fully independent as specified in the Constitution of the Federal

---

[35] *House of Representatives Debates on Federation of Nigeria, August 20, 1960, cols 2669 – 71.*
[36] *Constitution of the Federal Republic of Nigeria, 1999. Powers of the Federal Republic of Nigeria.*
[37] *Nigerian Annual Budget // Premium Times. October 10, 2018.*

Republic of Nigeria 1999, as amended, due to the foundation on which the institutions were laid.

Moreover, the three major institutions responsible for the formulation and implementation of Nigeria's foreign policy are the Ministry of Foreign Affairs (MFA)[38], the Presidential Advisory Council on International Relations (PACIR)[39], and the Nigerian Institute of International Affairs[40].

The Ministry of Foreign Affairs is the statutory organ of the Nigerian government and is charged with the primary responsibility for the formulation, articulation, conduct, and execution of Nigeria's foreign policy, as well as the management of the country's external relations. The Ministry started as a small unit in the External Affairs Division office of Prime Minister Tafawa Balewa, which was responsible for the conduct of foreign and Commonwealth relations.

The Ministry has been redistributed according to Nigeria's foreign policy objectives and functions under its current mandate 31 (Ofoegbu, 1990). For example, the 1999 Constitution of the Federal Republic of Nigeria, as amended, specified the goals and objectives of the Ministry. According to Chapter II, Section 19, of the 1999 Constitution, the Ministry of Foreign Affairs is obliged to implement the diplomatic principles of state policies, laws, and regulations. It is also saddled with the responsibility of drafting policy plans, laws, and regulations for its diplomatic work. However, the Ministry, from its inception, has been maintaining the status quo in the formation and implementation of foreign policy, retaining the Afrocentric foreign policy concept irrespective of various foreign policy concepts introduced by different administrations.

The Ministry's mandate, as approved in the 2007 Reforms, was dedicated to the vigorous pursuit of the vital national interests of the Federal Republic of Nigeria and the promotion of African integration and unity, international cooperation for the consolidation of global

---

[38] *Nigeria Ministry of Foreign Affairs. Great Nation, United in Diversity.*
[39] *Presidential Advisory Council on International Relations.*
*Institutional Processes of Foreign Policy: Foreign Policy Making and Implementation in Nigeria.*
[40]*Nigerian Institute of International Affairs.URL: http://www.niianet.org. (accessed on:21.04.2021).*

peace, security, a just world economic order, democratic values, etc. (Ministry of Foreign Affairs Annual Report, 2012)[41].

It is imperative to mention that the office of the Presidency oversees the activities of the Honourable Minister of Foreign Affairs, who in return gives directives to senior officials in the departments and Nigerian missions abroad, such as embassies, consulates, and general and permanent missions located in Geneva, Vienna, and New York, on the implementation of foreign policy.

There are also departments for bilateral and multilateral issues in the Ministry of Foreign Affairs. For instance, the African bilateral affairs department oversees and regulates the activities of all 55 African countries in line with the foreign policy guidelines. The African Multilateral Affairs Department oversees the activities of the African Union, the Economic Community of the West African States, the East African Community, the Southern African Development Community, etc. The Sub-Regional Organisations Division addresses the Gulf of Guinea Commission (GGC), Lake Chad Basin Commission (LCBC), and Niger Basin Authority (NBA).

Accordingly, these departments also create several policy divisions, such as the foreign service inspectorate, research and statistics, procurement, staff, training, welfare, information, and communications technology. In the international organisation department are the First United Nations and Second United Nations Divisions, which deal with the United Nations, Commonwealth of Nations, Organisation of Petroleum Exporting Countries (OPEC), and other global international organisations to which Nigeria belongs. In the Department of Administration are divisions such as Appointment, Employment, Promotion, Deployment and Discipline, Finance, Accounts, Salaries and Allowances, and External and Internal Audit, among others. In the Department of Consular are the Immigration, Legal, and Treaties Divisions.

The Federal Republic of Nigeria's quest to strengthen and consolidate its foreign policy has necessitated the creation of an embassy abroad. Currently, Nigeria has 109 embassies, high commissions, and the Consulate–General of Nigeria in various countries representing Nigeria; furthermore, officers or foreign

---

[41] *Ministry of Foreign Affairs Annual Report, 2012. Abuja Nigeria.*

missions who are responsible for the affairs of Nigerians abroad are posted from the Ministry of Foreign Affairs, the Federal Ministry of Defence[42], the Nigeria Immigration Service[43], and the Accountant General of the Federation[44].

Foreign Service officers, administrative attaches, finance attaches, defence attaches, immigration attaches, and other domestic staff are among the categories of officers posted to represent Nigerian missions. All the categories of officers mentioned are under Ambassador or Consul– General, who is the head of mission. The mission has various departments or sections, such as administration, political, economic, trade and investment, consular, immigration, visa and passport, and in some missions' defense section[45]. The Nigerian missions abroad send their reports and correspondences to their various government offices in Abuja and especially to the Ministry of Foreign Affairs. Foreign policy decision-making by the Nigerian government has contributed to the development of the foreign policy of Nigeria and Africa by extension. The MDAs are responsible for carrying out the laws and implementing policies of the Federal Republic of Nigeria and also represent the country in meetings organised by international organisations, such as the African Union (AU), Economic Community of West African States (ECOWAS), Gulf of Guinea Commission (GGC)[46], Lake Chad Basin Commission (LCBC)[47], Niger Basin Authority (NBA)[48], Food and Agriculture Organisation (FAO)[49], International Labour Organisation (ILO)[50], International Civil Aviation Organisation (ICAO)[51], World Bank, International Monetary Fund (IMF)[52], etc.

They are also allowed to represent the country in inter-ministerial meetings organised by the ministry of foreign affairs, where they are briefed and presented with policy documents. In most cases, they

---

[42] *Federal Ministry of Defence. Federal Republic of Nigeria.*
[43] *Nigeria Immigration Service. Federal Republic of Nigeria.*
[44] *Accountant General of the Federation. Federal Republic of Nigeria.*
[46] *Gulf of Guinea Commission.*
[47] *Lake Chad Basin Commission.*
[48] *Niger Basin Authority*
[49] *Food and Agriculture Organization.*
[50] *International Labour Organization.*
[51] *International Civil Aviation Organization.*
[52] *World Bank, International Monetary Fund.*

deliberate and agree on the subject before representing the country abroad. For example, the Federal Ministry of Agriculture and Rural Development (FMARD) is responsible for the agricultural sector of the Nigerian economy. The agricultural transformation agenda can be achieved by growing the sector, providing food, and generating employment that can transform the country into a leading global market.[53].

Nevertheless, the Ministry represents Nigeria at meetings organised by FAO and other related international organisations with a prepared mindset to secure and protect the integrity of the country and Africa in general. Moreover, the ministry relates to ICAO and IMO, among other international organisations on matters relating to Nigeria's foreign policy in Africa.

The Federal Ministry of Defence has contributed to African foreign policy in a number of areas. The Ministry was established on October 1, 1958, and has the statutory responsibility of overseeing the defence profile of Nigeria from the perspective of the Armed Forces. The ministry regulates and supervises the operations of the Defence Headquarters and Services, namely, the Army, Navy, and Air Force, as well as Tri–Service Institutions/Parastatals[54]. More importantly, the ministry has been attending meetings with countries and international organizations, such as the African Union (AU), Economic Community of West African States (ECOWAS), Gulf of Guinea Commission (GGC), Lake Chad Basin Commission (LCBC), and Niger Basin Authority (NBA), on the issues of security and defence.

Since the inception of the Federal Ministry of Education in 1988, Nigeria has been using the platform to promote the educational system in West Africa[55], which has contributed greatly to the growth of African foreign policy. The ministry is responsible for all training, innovation, teaching, and offering scholarships to Nigerian citizens. The Ministry represents Nigeria at meetings of the AU, ECOWAS, United Nations Educational Scientific and Cultural Organisation (UNESCO)[56], and other international organisations that deal with education.

---

[53] *Federal Ministry of Agriculture and Rural Development.*
[54] *Federal Ministry of Defence. Federal Republic of Nigeria.*
[55] *Federal Ministry of Education. Federal Republic of Nigeria.*
[56] *United Nations Educational, Scientific and Cultural Organization.*

Another ministry that has contributed greatly to African foreign policy is the Federal Ministry of Interior[57]. Nigerian citizenship, immigration services, business permits, and expatriate quotas are some of the things that the ministry is obligated to grant. The ministry has maintained the free visa policy for ECOWAS[58]. The ministry comprises customs, immigration, police, and paramilitary services. Since their inception, these ministries have been representing Nigeria at meetings relating to issues of peace and security in the AU, ECOWAS, GGC, LCBC, NBA, and other international organisations, most especially with countries that share borders with Nigeria.

The Federal Ministry of Justice[59] has been observing the ECOWAS, AU, and international norms in discharging its duty. The ministry at every point ensures that the rule of law prevails and that justice is accessible to all, irrespective of the personalities involved. The Ministry has the statutory mandate to oversee eight government parastatals, such as the Nigerian Law Reform Commission,[60] the Council of Legal Education[61], the National Drug Law Enforcement Agency (NDLEA),[62] and the National Agency for the Prohibition of Trafficking in Persons (NAPTIP)[63]. The ministry has been involved in a number of capacities, such as negotiating and vetting contract agreements, as well as participating in bilateral and multilateral relations on behalf of the Federal Republic of Nigeria.[64].

The Federal Ministry of Women Affairs and Social Development (FMWASD) was established in 1989. The ministry is saddled with responsibilities to advise the government on gender and children's issues and issues affecting individuals with disabilities and the elderly[65]. The ministry has been representing Nigeria at international meetings

---

[57] *Federal Ministry of Interior. Federal Republic of Nigeria.*
[58] *Supplementary Protocol A/SP.2/5/90 on the implementation of the Third Phase, Right to Establishment of the Protocol on Free Movement. Right of Residence and Establishment.1990.*
[59] *Federal Ministry of Justice. Federal Republic of Nigeria.*
[60] *Nigerian Law Reform Commission. Federal Republic of Nigeria.*
[61] *Council of Legal Education. Institute of Advanced Legal Studies.*
[62] *National Drug Law Enforcement Agency. Federal Republic of Nigeria.*
[63] *National Agency for the Prohibition of Trafficking in Persons. Federal Republic of Nigeria.*
[64] *Federal Ministry of Justice. Federal Republic of Nigeria.*
[65] *Federal Ministry of Women Affairs and Social Development. Federal Republic of Nigeria.*

on issues of gender and cultural adaptation, especially with countries that share borders with Nigeria. The Ministry also initiates policy guidelines and leads the process of ensuring gender equality and mainstreaming at both the national and international levels for the benefit of the African continent.

The Federal Ministry of Petroleum Resources has an obligation to regulate and implement policies in the oil and gas sector. The ministry also oversees the activities of stakeholders and agencies such as the Nigerian National Petroleum Corporation (NNPC)[66], the Petroleum Technology Development Fund (PTDF)[67], and the Department of Petroleum Resources (DPR)[68] in order to ensure compliance with all applicable laws and regulations in oil and gas[69]. The ministry has been representing Nigeria at meetings organised by petroleum sectors such as OPEC[70] and other international organisations.

The Federal Ministry of Youth and Sports Development (FMYSD) is responsible for coordinating, planning, researching, training, monitoring, and evaluating projects. In addition, the Ministry represents Nigeria at meetings organised for youth and sports in the West African Football Union (WAFU)[71], Confederation of African Football (CAF)[72], Federation of International Football Association (FIFA)[73], and International Olympic Committee (IOC)[74], among other sporting international organisations in the world that Nigeria participates in. The Federal Republic of Nigeria has been using the platform to unite African youth[75] and promotion of African foreign policy.

Former President Olusegun Obasanjo in 2001 established he Presidential Advisory Council on International Relations was and it comprises renowned Nigerian diplomats and experts whose main goal is to provide alternative policy options to the president.

---

[66] *Nigerian National Petroleum Corporation. Federal Republic of Nigeria.*
[67] *Petroleum Technology Development Fund. Federal Republic of Nigeria.*
[68] *Department of Petroleum Resources. Federal Republic of Nigeria.*
[69] *Federal Ministry of Petroleum Resources. Federal Republic of Nigeria.*
[70] *Organization of the Petroleum Exporting Countries. Federal Republic of Nigeria.*
[71] *West African Football Union.*
[72] *Confederation of African Football.*
[73] *Federation of International Football Association.*
[74] *International Olympic Committee.*
[75] *Federal Ministry of Youth and Sports. Federal Republic of Nigeria.*

The Nigerian Institute of International Affairs (NIIA) was established in 1961 but adopted in May 1963. Its primary objectives are to encourage and facilitate understanding of international relations based on the circumstances, conditions, and relations of foreign countries and their peoples. Since its founding, the institute has held conferences, roundtables and lectures. The institute's aims are to resolve foreign policy issues and serve as an instrument of foreign policy formulation in Nigeria. It also serves as an intellectual base upon which decision-makers rely for informed opinion and expert advice to make rational choices between contending policy options.

Finally, the impact of Nigeria's foreign policy institutions on Africa has been remarkable in all ramifications; from the above narratives, Nigeria's institutional system has contributed immensely to promoting African foreign policy. Since Nigeria gained independence in 1960, its foreign policy institutions have been devoted to the development of Africa in line with Nigeria's foreign policy objectives and national interests.

### 1.7 Afrocentrism in Nigeria's Foreign Policy

Solidarity and cooperation with African states have always been essential elements of Nigeria's foreign policy. Nigeria's first Prime Minister, Tafawa Balewa, in his submission to the United Nations General Assembly in 1961[76], expressed Nigeria's desire to work with other African countries for the progress of Africa and to help in bringing all African territories to a state of responsible independence (Enikanolaiye, 2013). In line with this, the Nigerian government articulated plans focusing purely on African affairs.

It is imperative to note that Nigeria has taken a position as a mouthpiece and reliable defender of Africa's interest in the international community, especially concerning the issues of decolonisation of Africa and the struggle against apartheid. Nigeria's effort and role in ending racism and other crimes against humanity in South Africa were undeniable. The issue of Africa's decolonization has been a fundamental aspect of Nigeria's foreign policy to assist and influence within the limits of its resources (Gambari, 1997).

---

[76] *Maiden General Assembly Statement at the United Nations.*

---

Since its foreign policy formation, Nigeria has centred its foreign policy on Africa, using the concept of Afrocentrism to improve its relations with African states. However, it was believed that the leadership style laid down by the founding fathers necessitated the Afrocentric foreign policy concept. As a country that aspires to be first among equals on the African continent, Nigeria has consistently exercised its diplomatic muscle to advance the interests of fellow African countries (Nwalie, 2020). Nigeria, since its independence, has entered into several bilateral and multilateral agreements with different nations of the world and international organisations to advance certain objectives in line with its national interests[77].

However, many scholars and concerned Africans have argued that Nigeria's Afrocentric foreign policy is not driven by its national interest but by an obscure consideration of the morality and welfare of its neighbors. According to David (1973), foreign policy is determined by a number of factors, including geo-demographic, economic, and military means, which are all components of national interest. In other words, Nigeria's Afrocentric foreign policy is associated with its national interests. Thus, Nigeria's Afrocentric foreign policy was geared to actualize its national interests and foreign policy objectives, which is paramount to the state of Nigeria in interacting with the community of nations for mutual benefit.

For instance, Chapter II, Section 19, of the 1999 constitution of Nigeria highlights the following: (1) promotion of the national interest; (2) promotion of African integration and support of African unity; (3) promotion of international cooperation for the consolidation of universal peace and mutual respect among all nations and the elimination of discrimination in all its manifestations; (4) respect for international law and treaty obligations; (5) settlement of international disputes by negotiation, mediation, conciliation, arbitration, and adjudication; and (6) promotion of a just world economic order[78].

To a greater extent, Nigeria's Afrocentric foreign policy has helped in the consolidation and promotion of good neighbourliness.

---

[77] *Official Document of the Ministry of Foreign Affairs, Abuja on Nigeria's Bilateral and Multilateral Relations with the world.*

[78] *Official Gazette, Federal Republic of Nigeria 1999 Constitution (as amended) with the National Industrial Court .98. (20). Government Notice No.103, The Federal Government Printer, Lagos, FGP 027/32011/2, 200 (OL13)*

Demographic, political, and economic reasons are some of the factors associated with the development of the policy related to security matters in Nigeria.

However, many academicians have tried to justify the subject using components of Nigeria's national interest and economic influence. Accordingly, proponents argue that Nigeria's Afrocentric policy has been driven without any specific interest in connection to the country's domestic interests and economic woes. Others claimed that Nigeria's rich socioeconomic and military capacity has made it possible for the country to always intervene in conflict settlement within its immediate sub-region and Africa.

Akinyemi's (1987) doctrine of «Reciprocity in Nigeria's Foreign Policy» documented various components of the country's national security interests and their systemic relationship. It was argued that Reciprocity in Nigeria's Foreign Policy was the first serious effort made in identifying and defining Nigeria's national interests in political, economic, social, and security terms.

In the context of good neighbourliness, the Afrocentric foreign policy showed that Nigeria owes some measures of responsibility to its neighbours and Africa. This was amplified by Nigeria's former foreign affairs minister, Bolaji Akinyemi, to the effect that Nigeria has responsibilities to Africa (Akinterinwa, 2001). This means there is sufficient justification to support consideration for good neighbourliness in Africa.

In a statement made by Nigeria's first Prime Minister, Tafawa Balewa, on 7 October 1960, at the United Nations General Assembly, justifying Nigeria's Afrocentric foreign policy and good neighbourliness, he said that Nigeria would be paying more attention to the problems of Africa in comparison to the rest of the world. According to him, any human would first secure and protect its immediate neighbours before attending to the outside world[79].

The integrity and welfare of Nigeria and its neighbours have been promoted and protected by this (Ogunnubi, 2018). All of this was in

---

[79] *Statement by Abubakar Tafawa Balewa. Prime Minister of the Federal Republic of Nigeria at the United Nations General Assembly, New York, October 7, 1960. Maiden General Assembly Statement at the United Nations.*

---

Chapter One | George Awele Nwalie and Yao Nikez Adu

tandem and in consonance with Nigeria's first Prime Minister's ideas to be commensurate with Nigeria's name and status as a 'messiah' of the continent (Claude, 1964). The concept of Afrocentric and good neighbourliness was emphasised when Jaja Anucha Wachuku, the Nigerian first Minister of Foreign Affairs, declared that any Nigeria's foreign policy that does not connote the interest of the common man on the continent of Africa is unrealistic. According to him, charity begins at home; thus, the dividend of Nigeria's foreign policy should be seen in the affairs of the people.

Despite the cultural, linguistic, and economic barriers caused by African colonial masters, Nigeria has succeeded in promoting peace, prosperity, stability, and development. Nigeria's has also recorded successes in the promotion of political goodwill and mutual understanding among African countries, and it has used its diverse cultural inheritance as a tool for strengthening diplomatic ties among African states.

For instance, Nigeria has signed various bilateral and multilateral investments, taxation, and immigration treaties, which also include conventions, memoranda of understanding, and agreements[80]. Nigeria has a bilateral agreement on cooperation, meetings on the Joint Commission, and Treaties of Friendship and Cooperation, especially with those African nations where it has an abolition of visa agreements (Okochi, 1990). However, the agreements allow nationals of the affected countries to enter Nigeria without visas and vice versa. In particular, the agreements only apply to people who are allowed to stay in Nigeria for 90 days, while those in agreement with Nigeria or intending to work must submit to the specific country's Immigration Act[81].

These agreements contained negotiable protocols on how to move these countries forward, especially on issues of economic, financial, and customs matters, frontier exchanges, free movement of persons

---

[80] *Treaty of the Economic Community of West African States. Treaties / Agreements / Charters / Protocols / Conventions / Declarations.1993.*
[81] *Supplementary Protocol on the Code of Conduct for the Implementation of the Protocol on Free Movement of Persons, the Right of Residence and Establishment.1985.*

and goods, cultural and technical matters, rights of establishment, and judicial and legal assistance conferences[82].

However, most terms and conditions of the agreement have been violated. For instance, in Nigeria-South Africa relations, the issue of xenophobia has remained a constant irritant. The effect of xenophobic attacks on African migrants in poor neighbourhoods in Cape Town, Durban, and Johannesburg in 2008, 2015, and 2019[83] instigated several African countries, such as Nigeria, Zambia, and others, to boycott the Africa economic summit in 2019 in Cape Town, South Africa. This led to the closure of the South African embassy in most of the affected states[84].

---

[82]*Supplementary Protocol A/SP.2/5/90 on the implementation of the Third Phase, Right to Establishment of the Protocol on Free Movement. Right of Residence and Establishment.1990.*
[83]*South Africa migrant attacks // Aljazeera, 4 Sep, 2019.*
[84]*South Africa closes embassy in Nigeria // France, 5 Sep, 2019.*

# Chapter Two

## The Dynamics of Nigeria's Foreign Policy

### 2.1 Nigeria's Foreign Policy in Africa

The Africanist movement of 1893 galvanised the civilised and educated people of African descent in the diaspora against the established order of European colonialism, racism, slavery, and apartheid (Victor et al., 2020). The root of Pan-Africanism can be traced back to the brutality of slavery in the Americas and the Caribbean people of African origin, who had been born in captivity since 1787[85]. For emphasis, Pan-Africanism began as a movement and ideology, situating its relevance to the encouragement of Africans to key into the pursuit of unity and solidarity among black people all over the globe.

Pan-Africanism has been viewed by scholars as vital, with a connection to the economic, social, and political advancement of black people while also asserting and insisting on the uniformity of fate and destiny of African peoples within and outside the continent (Victor et al., 2020).For instance, Nnamdi Azikiwe, the first President of Nigeria, proposes in his 1962 address on the future of Pan-Africanism that Pan-Africanism should be concretised either in the form of regional states or one continental state, whichever is feasible, allowing this to be done voluntarily without upsetting the total sovereignty of the states concerned[86].

The Pan-African Movement became a roadmap for the formation of Nigeria's foreign policy. The West African region was the centre of pan-Africanism in Africa. However, Nigeria, since independence has walked the path of pan-Africanism and the right of all peoples to self-determination, and its foreign policy is based on its continued survival, security, and well-being, as well as regional, continental, and universal

---

[85] *The History of Pan-Africanism. New Internationalist, 2000.*
[86] *Statement by Nnamdi Azikiwe. First President of Nigeria. The Future of Pan-Africanism. Black Past. 2009.*

peace and security and the principles of the UN Charter[87]. Pan-Africanism, which influenced their social and political engagements, contributed to the decision-making process in Nigeria.

Pan-Africanism encourages Nigeria's foreign policy objectives. Nnamdi Azikiwe and Herbert Macaulay were influenced by the objectives of Pan-Africanism; in turn, they incorporated these objectives into Nigeria's foreign policy to encourage anti-colonialism[88]. Many other Nigerians of Brazilian and West Indian backgrounds had previously encountered Pan-Africanism, which influenced their social and political engagements and contributed to the decision-making process in Nigeria.

Nnamdi Azikiwe, the first President of Nigeria, defined pan-Africanism as the unity of newly independent African states. Capitalism, colonialism, and imperialism deprived Africa of its wealth and its will to live as a human being, even though he believed that slavery played a role in depopulating Africa[89]. He believed that Africans needed to restore their dignity before they could try to revive their stature in the Council of Nations.

The framing of its foreign policy objectives and principles was affected by the historical inclusion of Pan-Africanism into the political and ideological structures of Nigeria. Nigerian foreign policy was founded on the eradication of colonialism and other forms of exploitation, domination, oppression, and marginalisation of Africans. In line with this judgement, Nigeria started a foreign policy concept called Africa as the centrepiece of Nigeria's foreign policy.

The pan-Africanism feature that has expressed enthusiasm for the formation of the United States of Africa is part of Nigeria's desire for continental unity and harmonious co-existence. Since independence, Nigeria's foreign policy objectives have been centred on promoting continental political unity, which is among the features of pan-

---

[87] *Despite challenges, Nigeria's foreign policy stays its Pan – Africanist course // Vanguard News, August 21, 2021.*

[88] *Pine A. Pan-Africanism And Nigeria's Foreign Policy: Some Contemporary Notes // Modern Ghana News, an Internet Publication. December 16, 2020.*

[89] *Statement by Nnamdi Azikiwe. First President of Nigeria. The Future of Pan – Africanism. Black Past. 2009.*

Africanism[90]. However, pan-Africanism is a critical element in Nigeria's foreign policy, which has shaped, encouraged, and centred Nigeria's foreign policy on African affairs. Nevertheless, the only panacea to end imperialism, neo-colonialism, apartheid, racism, underdevelopment, and white supremacy is for African leaders to jointly institute a national development entity that would adopt and implement a unified concept for the African continent.

## 2.2 Nigeria in the AU

**The African Union.** The calls for the transmutation of the Organisation of African Unity (OAU) to the African Union (AU) became inevitable due to the inability of the organisation to maintain its principles and objectives[91]. Oftentimes, the OAU was criticised for not being able to ensure good governance within African countries and for being unable to provide diplomatic and political solutions to conflicts across the continent. According to Dunmoye (2011) "the critics and cynics of OAU often go to the extent of castigating the organisation as a toothless bulldog". President Olusegun Obasanjo, in his report at the African Union Twenty-First Ordinary Session in Addis Ababa, Ethiopia, in 2013, reiterated that the main vision for transforming the Organisation of African Unity (OAU) into the African Union (AU) was to enable Africa to redress the economic, social, and political challenges confronting the continent[92].

Nonetheless, the issue of noninterference in the affairs of another state, which is among the key principles of the OAU charter, was identified as a major setback related to organisational performance. Again, on the issues of dispute settlement among member states, the OAU was criticised for its role, which was limited to mediating between disputants and has no power to impose a collective will on

---

90 *Official Gazette, Federal Republic of Nigeria 1999 Constitution (as amended) with the National Industrial Court. 98 (20). Government Notice No.103, The Federal Government Printer, Lagos, FGP 027/32011/2, 200 (OL13).*

91 *Ibid*

92 *President Olusegun Obasanjo. Statement Assembly of the Union Twenty-First Ordinary Session in Addis Ababa, Ethiopia. Assembly/AU/6(XXI) Original: English. SC10056. 2013.*

disobedient members. For instance, the OAU meditative role does not produce instant remedies to feuds, as evidenced by the prolongation and persistence of the Congo crises. According to Saliu (2013), the OAU failed to play a fundamentally decisive role because its members were passionately split over the politics of the Congo crisis, which in turn prolonged and affected its role and performance in the crisis.

Subsequently, after enduring some of the bloodiest resistance to independence, many leaders saw the OAU as a threat to the sovereignty of their young states. The charter of the OAU, which was signed on May 25, 1963, in Addis Ababa, Ethiopia, reflected the compromise between the radical and moderate groups[93]. The OAU was prohibited from interference in internal state matters, which often made it an impotent bystander to many violations of human rights under the rule of dictators such as the former President of Uganda, Idi Amin, and the former President of the Democratic Republic of the Congo, Mobutu Sese Seko.

Moreover, the failure of the OAU to maintain its principles and objectives was promised. African states called for the creation of the African Union (AU) at the extraordinary summit in Sirte, Libya, on September 9, 1999. However, the main objective for the transmutation of the Organisation of African Unity to the African Union (AU) was to shift from state-centred to people-centred interests[94]. Notwithstanding, the political climate in which the AU was born greatly contributed to the creation of the organisation. According to Vladimir (2014), the reform process adopted by the African Union is a positive step towards continental and regional integration. On this, Nigusie & Savicheva (2020) argued that Gaddafi M.'s involvement in the transformation of the OAU into the AU was a result of Libyan foreign policy, which intensified in Sub-Saharan Africa; nevertheless, they claimed that the pan-Arabism of M. Gaddafi gave way to pan-Africanism.

In addition, the desire of Muammar Ghaddafi of Libya, Olusegun Obasanjo of Nigeria, and Thabo Mbeki of South Africa to revive the spirit of African unity contributed to the materialisation of the AU.

---

[93] *OAU Charter, The Addis Ababa Treaty of 1963. Refworld.*
[94] *OAU/AU Treaty.*

Thabo Mbeki, Muammar Gaddafi, and Olusegun Obasanjo became the leading figures in the move towards the AU (Nwalie, 2020). In this light, Kosukhin (2001) argued that the approach and behaviour of the leaders on the continent of Africa towards the usual hijacking of political power and its process in the various African states are seen and referred to as a complex system of social relations.

Nevertheless, the successful creation of the AU was made possible due to the commitment and sacrifices of major actors such as Muammar Ghaddafi of Libya, Olusegun Obasanjo of Nigeria, Thabo Mbeki of South Africa, Abdoulaye Wade of Senegal, and Bouteflika of Algeria, who are tired of the achievements recorded by the OAU (Oshewolo, 2019). President Olusegun Obasanjo of Nigeria and Thabo Mbeki of South Africa hijacked the project from President Muammar Ghaddafi to frustrate Libya's hegemonic ambitions and advance their hegemonic desires.

According to Fawole (2014), Nigeria's intellectual, philosophical, and ideological contributions to the theory and praxis of African integration were acknowledged during President Obasanjo's speeches at different African and extra-African forums. While Tieku (2004) argued that President Obasanjo's rhetoric was intended to persuade African leaders to accept his ideas and advance Nigeria's historic role as the giant of Africa, promoting solidarity, security, and development.

For more emphasis on President Olusegun Obasanjo's ideologies towards OAU/AU affairs the analytical evidence presented by Kayode Shinkaiye, Nigeria's ambassador to Ethiopia and permanent representative to the OAU/AU from 2000 to 2003, shows that the Nigerian Embassy in Addis Ababa, in partnership with the Ministry of Foreign Affairs under the leadership of Alhaji Sule Lamido, engaged actively in drawing up all the instruments establishing the AU.

Again, Wapmuk (2014) argued that President Olusegun Obasanjo's active role in the preparatory meetings that conceived the AU is to fulfill his leadership obligation as a member of the inner caucus together with countries such as Libya and South Africa. Although he claimed that Nigeria's high-level diplomacy was acknowledged in 2000 during the OAU heads of state and government summit in Lome, Togo.

Within the interval that the draft of the AU Constitutive Act was presented at the summit for deliberation and adoption, Presidents

Abdoulaye Wade of Senegal and Yoweri Museveni of Uganda proposed some amendments, which were not taken because of the feeling that revisiting the Constitutive Act could prevent its adoption at the summit. However, President Olusegun Obasanjo argued that the Constitutive Act of the AU was not a perfect document but sufficiently represented all shades of opinion within the African continent. He suggested the adoption of the AU Constitutive Act, and it was given consent to almost immediately (Oshewolo, 2019).

For emphasis, the African Affairs Department of the Ministry of Foreign Affairs and the Embassy of Nigeria in Addis Ababa, in view of perfecting the legal proceedings for the establishment of the AU , requested the deployment of a lawyer from the Ministry to Addis Ababa to help the Embassy take care of the legal contents of its activities concerning the transformation of the OAU to the AU (Akinsanya, 2014)

In line with this judgment, the Nigerian Embassy was able to produce, between November and December 2001, its own draft rules of procedure for the Assembly, the Executive Council, and the Permanent Representatives Committee, as well as the Statute for the Commission and the draft protocol for the Peace and Security Council. According to Tieku (2004), the process leading to the transmutation of OAU to AU was defined by a clash of interests among major actors, which automatically influenced the system of operation after establishment.

Despite that, Nigeria's position prevailed. For instance, President Muammar Ghaddafi, in 1999, during the process of OAU replacement, proposed a more radical approach that would lead to the establishment of the United States of Africa. It was believed that President Muammar Ghaddafi wanted to use the opportunity to cement his full return to the geopolitics of black Africa and to demonstrate his renewed commitment to the pan–Africanism objective.

Muammar Ghaddafi's diplomatic moves in this regard were checked by the likes of Presidents Olusegun Obasanjo of Nigeria and Thabo Mbeki of South Africa, who never wanted him to succeed in his pursuit. Although President Olusegun Obasanjo gave his consent to the Muammar Ghaddafi proposal, he adopted a more pragmatic approach to the issue of African integration. For clarity, President Olusegun Obasanjo made a persuasive argument in favour of incrementalism and gradualism as Africans march towards integration during the 1999 OAU Summit in Sirte, Libya.

Apparently, the adoption culminated in the 2002 Summit in Durban, South Africa, where the formation of the AU was officially announced to the world, immediately after the disbandment of the OAU on 9 July 2002. According to Akinsanya O. (2014), the African leaders converged in the South African city of Durban on 9 July 2002, to form a successor pan–African Organisation to rekindle the spirit of pan–Africanism, which was believed to be the only panacea to promote African unity.

Finally, President Muhammadu Buhari of Nigeria at the 34th Summit of the AU, which was held virtually in 2021, called for a comprehensive reform of the structures and operations of the African Union to make it more functional in meeting targets, warning that the organisation would become stale unless it became more result–oriented[95]. President Muhammadu Buhari commended President Paul Kagame of Rwanda for presenting a special report on the need to reform the AU. He believed that his leadership demands a truly reformed, efficient, and effective AU Commission, one that is fully committed to the discharge of its duties and responsibilities.

The calls for the transmutation of the Organisation of African Unity to the African Union were necessitated because the OAU was consistently unable to address the challenges facing the continent. The process for the OAU transmutation to AU started with the unanimous will of member states, who generally adopted the motion for the establishment of AU at the fifth Extraordinary Summit of the AU held in Sirte, Libya, from 1 to 2 March 200.[96]

**Impact of Nigeria's Foreign Policy on African Economic Initiatives.** Due to Nigeria's regional hegemonic status, the country is positioned to play a vital role in the economic initiatives of Africa.

---

[95] *Muhammadu Buhari Calls for Reform of African Union // Premium Times, February 7, 2021.*

[96] *Special Motion of Thanks to the Leader of the Great Socialist Libya Arab Jamahiriya Brother Muammar Al Ghaddafi Adopted by the Fifth Extraordinary Session of the Assembly of Heads of State and Government. United Nations General Assembly. A/55/951. 2001.*

Nigeria's economic policy and its national interests, which are centred on Africa, have encouraged the country to cooperate with other African states in pursuing African economic initiatives, such as the New Partnership for Africa's Development (NEPAD) economic initiatives. The New Partnership for Africa's Development (NEPAD) is an African-led strategy for economic development and a poverty eradication initiative for the African continent[97].

NEPAD was adopted by the African Heads of State and Government of the Organisation of African Unity (OAU) in 2001 and ratified by the African Union (AU) in 2002 to tackle Africa's development problems within the continent. The core mandate of NEPAD is to eradicate poverty, reposition Africa on the path of sustainable development, terminate marginalisation in Africa, and empower women[98]. NEPAD's five initiating countries are Algeria, Egypt, Nigeria, Senegal, and South Africa, and 15 members are elected based on the AU's five regions, usually for two-year terms[99].

NEPAD aims to provide an overarching vision and policy framework for accelerating economic cooperation and integration among African countries. NEPAD's four primary objectives are as follows:

1. to eradicate poverty,
2. promote sustainable growth and development,
3. integrate Africa into the world economy,
4. accelerate the empowerment of women.

It is based on the underlying principles of a commitment to good governance, democracy, human rights, and conflict resolution, and the recognition that the maintenance of these standards is fundamental to the creation of an environment conducive to investment and long-term economic growth (Adams, 2006).

It is imperative to note that Nigeria played a vital role in the formation of NEPAD; without the involvement of Nigeria, the

---

[97] *The New Partnership for Africa's Development. Abuja, Nigeria. UN Human Rights Office of the High Commissioner. 2001.*
[98] *NEPAD. UN Department of Economic and Social Affairs Poverty.*
[99] *New Partnership for Africa's Development. AU.*

creation of NEPAD would have been more strenuous or unattainable. According to Adams (2006), the establishment of NEPAD was forecasted by Nigerian leaders on the belief that the regional document will reposition Africa on the path of long–term development, which will reduce its marginalisation in international economic relations.

Accordingly, former Nigerian President Olusegun Obasanjo, who lamented about African leadership, predicted that with the establishment of NEPAD, the whole of Africa's economy would grow while that of China, Europe, and North America would stagnate by 2025. He believed that the economic progress in Africa would continue to advance, making Africa a haven for investment, employment generation, and wealth creation by 2040. This was written by the Financial Times, Op-Ed titled My Africa Utopia[100].

Nigeria's involvement in NEPAD was believed to have encouraged and repositioned African economic relations in the international community in conformity with the Millennium Development Goals (MDGs)[101], as well as the Sustainable Development Goals (SDGs)[102], which attracted an urgent call for action by all countries, especially from the African continent, for a global economic partnership.

Subsequently, Nigeria believed that NEPAD represented a tacit recognition of the existence of a developmental crisis within the continent of Africa. To buttress this, Adams (2006) argued that the opportunities and economic interests of the regional initiative for African nations have been overstretched by African leaders and their Western allies, especially members of the G8 group, such as France, Germany, Italy, the United Kingdom, Japan, the United States, Canada, and Russia, who have pledged their support towards African economic development. According to Omoweh (2003), Nigeria is leading other African leaders in pursuing the mandate of NEPAD and ensuring the termination of every form of African marginalisation in the international community. While Ebegbulem (2012) argued that

---

[100] *Olusegun Obasanjo. My Africa Utopia. AUDA-NEPAD, African Union Development Agency. 2015.*
[101] *UN 2015 Agenda for Millennium Development Goals. MDG Success Springboard for New Sustainable Development Agenda: UN Report.*
[102] *UN 2030 Agenda for Sustainable Development Goals. Department of Economic and Social Affairs Sustainable Development.*

NEPAD is thus a commitment by African leaders to quicken the economic integration of the African continent into the global economy, as well as a call to the rest of the world to partner with the African continent.

On this premise, Wogu (2015) claimed that Nigeria became actively involved in African economic initiatives, such as the New Partnership for Africa's Development (NEPAD) and the African Peer Review Mechanism (APRM), because of its economic capacity. He believed that NEPAD initiatives were aimed at repositioning the course of Africa so that African states would see that the continent belonged to them and should take an active position in its development rather than look elsewhere.

Moreover, the idea of asking for assistance from development partners without wanting to take responsibility was to stop with the concept of NEPAD. By doing so, Africans would take responsibility for developing their continent on their own, as they have human and natural resources to promote growth on the continent. The development partners, when they see seriousness on the part of Africans, would be willing to assist the continent without the usual begging for assistance.

In line with the African Union's (AU) decision to improve the service delivery of NEPAD, President Muhammadu Buhari, on May 24, 2019, approved the transformation of the New Partnership for Africa's Development (NEPAD) into the African Union Development Agency–NEPAD (AUDA– NEPAD). It is believed that the mandate of the AUDA–NEPAD is to coordinate and execute regional and continental projects to promote regional integration towards the accelerated realisation of Agenda 2063[103].

Nigeria's role in NEPAD is embedded in its foreign policy principles, which encourage African economic initiatives. However, the NEPAD was created by Nigerians and the Republic of South Africa to eradicate poverty in Africa and to place African countries both individually and collectively on a path to sustainable growth and

---

[103]*President Muhammadu Buhari. Approves NEPAD's Transformation into AU Development Agency // Premium Times, May 24, 2019.*

development to halt the marginalisation of Africa in the globalisation process[104].

Finally, NEPAD is based on the principles of good governance as a basic requirement for peace, security, and sustainable political and socio-economic development. It is based on African ownership and the full utilisation of African resources for development. It rested on African ownership, leadership, and participation in all sectors of African society.

**African Union Agenda 2063.** The African Union economic initiative, AU Agenda 2063, was rooted in pan-Africanism and African Renaissance, which provide a robust framework for addressing past injustices and the realisation of the 21st century as the African century. The African heads of state and government signed the 50th Anniversary Solemn Declaration during the Golden Jubilee celebrations of the formation of the OAU/AU in May 2013 as an affirmation of their commitment to support Africa's new path for attaining inclusive and sustainable economic growth and development.

However, the declaration marked the dedication of Africa towards the attainment of the Pan-African vision of an integrated, prosperous, and peaceful Africa, driven by its citizens, representing a dynamic force in the international arena, and AU Agenda 2063 is the concrete manifestation of how the continent intends to achieve this vision within 50 years from 2013 to 2063[105].

The need to envision a long-term 50-year development trajectory for Africa is important, as Africa needs to revise and adapt its development agenda due to ongoing structural transformations, increased peace and reduction in the number of conflicts, renewed economic growth and social progress, the need for people-centred development, gender equality, and youth empowerment, and the increased unity of Africa, which makes it a global power to be reckoned with and capable of rallying support around its common agenda.

---

[104]*Central Bank of Nigeria into NEPAD. Facts: 1/1/1900.*
[105] *AU 50th Anniversary Solemn Declaration Adopted by the 21st Ordinary Session of the Assembly of Heads of State and Government of the African Union, at Addis Ababa held on 26 May 2013.*

AU Agenda 2063 is initiated to consolidate the role of regional economic communities in rebuilding African economic relations. To accomplish this, the deliberate efforts of African leaders are required to nurture transformative leadership that will drive the agenda and defend African economic interests. Notwithstanding, Nigeria and other African countries aspirations for AU Agenda 2063 have reflected the desire for shared prosperity and economic well–being, for unity and integration, for a continent of free citizens and expanded horizons, where the full potential of women and youth, boys and girls and freedom from fear, disease, and want[106].

Subsequently, President Muhammadu Buhari of Nigeria, on 28 January 2018, during the opening ceremony of the 30th Assembly of Heads of State and Government of the African Union currently held at the AU headquarters in Addis Ababa, Ethiopia, declared Nigeria's intention to fight corruption on the continent. According to President Buhari, corruption is indeed one of the greatest evils on the African continent and should be approached in accordance with the African Union Agenda 2063. Under Aspiration 3, corruption erodes the development of a universal culture of good governance, democratic values, gender equality, respect for human rights, justice, and the rule of law.

Furthermore, AU Agenda 2063 is a vision designed by African leaders to eradicate poverty in the coming decades through enhanced investment in the productive capacities (skills and assets) of African people, improving incomes, creating jobs, and providing necessities of life, as well as transforming and growing the African economy through the beneficiation and value addition of natural resources[107]. AU Agenda 2063 encloses not only the African leaders' aspirations for the future of the continent but also recognises core flagship programmes that can promote African economic relations and development in order to promote African common identity through its history and cultural engagement.

Thus, Ogunbadejo (1980) believed that Nigeria played a primary role in facilitating the OAU's transition to the AU in 2002, the

[106] *Agenda 2063. African Union Commission, Popular Version, 03. 2015..*
[107] *Agenda 2063. African Union Commission, Popular Version, 03. 2015.*

establishment of the New Partnership for Africa's Development (NEPAD), the African Peer Review Mechanism (APRM), and AU Agenda 2063. As mentioned, these are institutions that have been playing a significant role in the administration and efficiency of Africa's reform economic processes.

On other issues vital to Nigeria as relating to African economic initiatives, Nigeria, as a leading state in Africa, is participating to make the AU Agenda 2063 of the Africa Union work. The agenda is based on African aspirations for development. The seven African Aspirations for AU Agenda 2063, according to the document, were derived through a consultative process with the African citizenry[108], and they are as follows:

1. A prosperous Africa, based on inclusive growth and sustainable development
2. An integrated continent, politically united, based on the ideals of Pan-Africanism and the vision of Africa's Renaissance
3. A peaceful and secure Africa
4. An Africa of good governance, democracy, respect for human rights, justice, and the rule of law
5. Africa with a strong cultural identity, common heritage, values, and ethics
6. An Africa whose development is people-driven, relying on the potential offered by people, especially its women and youth, and caring for children
7. Africa is a strong, united, resilient, and influential global player and partner.

However, the African Union intends to finance the project through its internal mechanism, with domestic resource mobilisation; in other words, the AU member countries will contribute at least 75% to 90% of the financing of AU Agenda 2063 on average per country. There is no doubt that Nigeria will be contributing hugely in relation to its annual contribution to the AU's regular budget (Bhaso et al., 2019). The African economic initiatives, AU Agenda 2063, have identified numerous benefits, such as sustainable peace, renewed economic

---

[108] *Ibid*

growth, and promotion of African unity, which were designed by Nigeria and other AU member states to reposition African economic relations in the international community. Nevertheless, these visions can only be attainable under the full implementation of Agenda 2063 aspirations, as mentioned earlier[109].

In line with this judgement, the government of Nigeria is spearheading the ongoing Abidjan-Lagos Coastal Corridor Project. Nigeria is leading the Abidjan-Lagos Coastal Corridor project which seeks to modernise the most heavily travelled ARTIN corridor in West Africa to facilitate trade and the movement of people and goods. The project includes the establishment of a one-stop border post and the enhancement of government capacities for PPP development and management. NEPAD facilitated this project through the provision of technical support to ECOWAS in the areas of project cycle management and the deployment of experts. The support enabled the countries to sign the project treaty in February 2014, which provides for a supranational corridor management authority and a seed fund contribution of US$50 million agreed[110].Nigeria is also among the countries that are involved in the 4500 km Algeria-Nigeria Optic Fibre project. The Algeria-Niger border segment has been completed and is operational but awaiting reinforcements carrying loop systems to ensure high network availability.

**Nigeria's Foreign Policy and Its Economic Well–Being.** Since independence, the guiding principles of Nigeria's foreign policy have remained enshrined in the 1999 Constitution, as amended in 2011, Chapter II, Article 19 of the Federal Republic of Nigeria Constitution[111]. These principles, together with Nigeria's national interest, have made it possible for Nigeria to centre its foreign policy concepts on African affairs. For instance, Nigeria's foreign policy core objectives have been the promotion of peace, economic cooperation and integration, development, and the fight against all forms of discrimination (Efem et al., 2014). These objectives have hugely

[109] *Central Bank of Nigeria into NEPAD. Facts: 1/1/1900.*
[110] Nigeria Role in AUDA-NEPAD. African Union Development Agency, key Result, 2022.
[111] *Nigeria's Constitution of 1999 with Amendments through 2011//Constituteproject. org.*

contributed to African economic initiatives as well as the economic well–being of African people.

On attaining independence, Prime Minister Alhaji Tafawa Balewa's administration laid the foundation for making Africa the centrepiece of Nigeria's foreign policy. This could be seen in his assertion on 7 October 1960, at the Plenary of the 15th Regular Session of the United Nations General Assembly, exactly six days after Nigeria gained independence and became the 99th member of the organisation that Nigeria belongs to Africa and Africa must claim first attention in Nigeria's external affairs, as regarding security and economic well–being of African people.

Subsequently, Nigeria's foreign policy instrument towards national and continental development is exceedingly complex and contentious. To buttress this, Efem et al. (2014) justified the discourse in the context of Nigeria's economic diplomacy side–by–side with Nigeria's bilateral and multilateral relations, basically, Nigerian economic relations that take place within and among states and non–state actors in the international arena.

This is not to argue that issues of international economic relations are mutually incompatible with Nigeria's foreign policy. Naturally, Nigeria's international economic relations and interactions are guided by its foreign policy objectives, which conform with its national interests. Under this purview, Nigeria's foreign policy is regarded as the action and inaction of the country towards other or nonstate actors within the international system to safeguard its national interests.

In this light, Alli (2010) says that Nigeria's foreign policy is not selfless but an apologist who comprises career foreign service officers, and a few scholars believe that Nigeria's foreign policy has yielded tangible and intangible results for the country since its formation in 1960. However, Nigeria's effort at reconstructing and transforming the economic well-being of its people through its economic initiatives requires a robust policy. Nigeria needs to identify the areas of concentration in pursuing its economic goals and objectives for the benefit of its people. Thus, Nigeria's foreign political policy must seek a positive alignment with its foreign economic interests to maximise the economic well-being of its people[112].

**Nigerian Economic Diplomacy in Africa.** Over the years, Nigeria has been using its economic diplomacy, such as hard and soft power resources, to protect economic security and attract foreign investment and project power, particularly within Africa. For instance, during Nigeria's economic recovery in 1975, Nigeria led other West African countries to establish ECOWAS. The Nigerian President, Yakubu Gowon, played a very decisive role in making sure that ECOWAS saw the light of the day. In addition, he pledged to be responsible for a full one-third of ECOWAS's financial needs (Ogunnubi et al., 2016). This was attainable and orchestrated because of the unexpected oil boom of the 1970s, which brought about a buoyant economy, in turn increasing the momentum for Nigeria's rising continental hegemony.

Nigeria's leadership role and economic prosperity during the period of ECOWAS creation offered the country a platform to pursue rigorous and active foreign policy. This is manifested in the leading role Nigeria played during the eradication of colonialism and white minority rule in countries such as Angola, Guinea–Bissau, Mozambique, Namibia, and South Africa, its aid to countries such as Angola, Benin, Botswana, Zambia, and Zimbabwe, and its peacekeeping mission in countries such as Liberia, Sierra Leone, and Democratic Republic of the Congo (Sanda, 2012).

It is crucial to note that Nigeria is the largest oil exporter in Africa and has the largest natural gas reserve on the continent. Africa has been benefiting from Nigeria's economic resources, which in turn has given Nigeria the economic will to contribute to African economic policy, especially in its subregion.

Again, Nigeria's significance is intrinsically tied to its economic diplomacy, particularly within the West and Central African subregions. In line with this judgment, Nigeria has been playing a dominant role in these subregions while also sustaining its responsibility and guiding principles of its foreign policy to protect and maintain peace among its contiguous states, which have remained

---

[112] *Nigeria's Constitution of 1999 with Amendments through 2011// Constituteproject.org.*

enshrined in the 1999 Constitution as amended in 2011, Chapter II, Article 19[113] of the Federal Republic of Nigeria Constitution.

Moreover, Nigeria has the economic and financial powers to assert influence on regional and continental levels. However, this substantial economic prowess has not only given Nigeria the free will to intervene in regional and continental conflicts to foster development, maintain political and economic stability, and encourage a dynamic foreign policy that has greatly impacted the growth and development of the continent of Africa (Amao, 2015).

It is clear that Nigeria's diplomatic behaviour is rooted in its economic diplomacy and prowess, which provide the country with an opportunity to play a subtle hegemonic role in the continent of Africa. For instance, Nigerian President Olusegun Obasanjo, among other African political leaders Muammar Ghaddafi of Libya and Thabo Mbeki of South Africa, pursued and became a leading figure in the move towards the transmutation of the Organisation of African Unity (OAU) to the African Union (AU) in 2002 (Nwalie, 2020). Additionally, Nigeria has been able to play a leading role on behalf of Africa in multilateral institutional arrangements such as the UN, the Organisation of African Unity (OAU, now the AU), and ECOWAS.

Finally, the lack of adequate infrastructure remains a critical constraint for economic growth and its stability in Nigeria, despite the huge efforts made by the successive Nigerian President, Ibrahim Babangida, to introduce the Structural Adjustment Programme (SAP)[114] to tackle Nigeria's financial challenges, etc., but to no avail. In line with this judgment, President Olusegun Obasanjo's initiated economic reform, which was meant to improve Nigeria's and Africa's capacity for economic growth and job creation, was considered inefficient[115]. However, Obasanjo's administration has been celebrated as one that helped restore Nigeria's status in the international system after a period of military authoritarian rule that earned the country a

---

[113] *Nigeria's Constitution of 1999 with Amendments through 2011 // Constituteproject.org.*

[114] *Nigeria. Structural Adjustment Programme: Policies, Implementation, and Impact // The World Bank. 1994.*

[115] *An interview with Olusegun Obasanjo: Up close and a little too personal // African Argument. September 28, 2017.*

negative foreign image. However, on the domestic front, the neoliberal economic reform programme of the administration was not popular among Nigerians. The impact of Nigeria's economic diplomacy on the economic well-being of its people has been insignificant. However, Nigeria needs to initiate a new domestic economic institution that will collaborate with international institutions or organisations, such as the World Trade Organisation, for efficient regulation of the flow of commodities.

**The African Continental Free Trade Impact on Nigeria's Economy.** While there is a general optimism around the promise of the newly in-force African Continental Free Trade Agreement (AfCFTA)[116]. The AFCFTA drops 90 percent of tariffs and includes policies aimed at eliminating nontariff barriers, such as customs delays. However, the aggregate long-term benefits of AfCFTA are likely to be substantial and larger than potential losses. Meanwhile, some countries and sectors will likely be negatively impacted in the short term.

Nigeria has the largest economy in Africa. On July 7, 2019, Nigeria signed the AfCFTA to become the 34th member of the trading group. Under the AfCFTA, Nigeria stands to gain from increased access to cheaper goods and services from other African countries, as its intra-African trade is currently low. Indeed, as of 2018, Nigeria's imports from the African region relative to total imports were 3.2 percent, while the share of Nigeria's exports to the African region relative to total exports was 13.2 percent. While, in 2020, Nigeria's main trading partner was actually China.

Estimating the impact of the AFCFTA on Nigeria, a tariff reduction enacted by one country has implications for its partners, suppliers, and competitors as it spills over to the rest of the world through trade networks and to other industries through supply chains. For instance, a reduction in tariffs on cotton production impacts the prices of textiles.

However, a regional tariff reduction is modelled as higher productivity, as it leads to a reduction in relative prices and has

---

[116] *Quantifying the impact on Nigeria of the African Continental Free Trade Area// Brookings. September 22, 2021.*

implications for the exchange of goods across countries and regions. In this framework, households and firms then purchase more imported articles at cheaper prices, raising trade volumes and increasing household welfare. For the same reason, changes in the relative prices of exports and imports induce higher demand for non-Nigerian-made products, depending on the variation in prices across sectors and countries.

Furthermore, Nigeria gains 1.55 percent in welfare. Decomposing welfare effects into effects due to change in volume of trade (1.14 percent) and effects due to change in terms of trade (0.14 percent) highlights the sources of Nigeria's positive gain by sector. As shown in Figure 1, agriculture, fishing, and other manufacturing industries account for 73 percent of the gains from volume of trade. A decline in export prices relative to import price. "Other manufacturing goods" account for most gains in terms of trade, while the agriculture and mining industries combined dilute gains by 32.6 percent.

**Figure 1: African Continental Free Trade impact on Nigeria economy: the volume of trade and terms of trade by sector.**

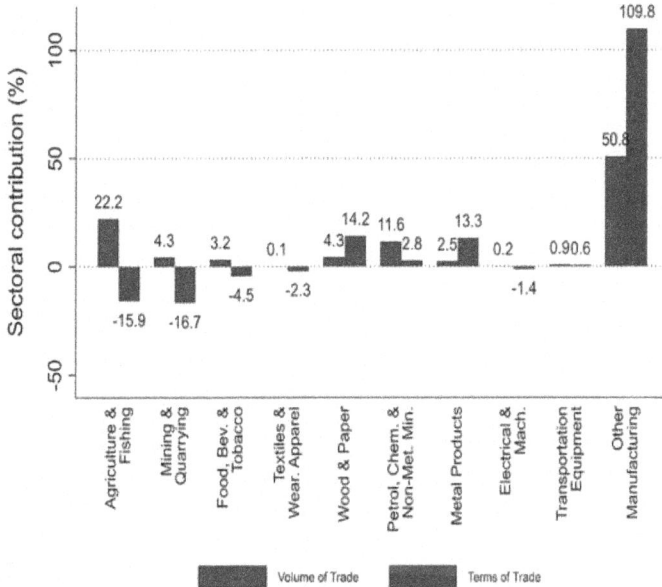

*Source: static computable, multisector, multicounty trade model version[1].*

However, the volume of trade; is sectoral trade relative to Nigeria's total trade, terms of trade are calculated as the difference in sectoral prices of exports and imports as a share of total price differences in all sectors. Welfare effects are the sum of the volume of trade (VOT) and terms of trade (TOT) effects. A negative TOT means the sector dilutes the positive gains. Sectoral contributions for TOT and VOT add up to 100 percent.

## 2.3 Nigeria and Her Contiguous Neighbours

Since independence in 1960, Nigeria has maintained strong relations with her contiguous neighbours, namely Benin, Niger, Chad, and Cameroon, as well as other countries in the West African subregion. With its involvement in issues of African decolonisation and its role in border and territorial dispute settlement, Nigeria has the free will to interact with its neighbors. (Sanda, 2012). According to Nwolise (1989), the Nigerian government established a strong relationship with its neighbours after gaining independence from Great Britain in 1960.

### Nigeria-Benin Republic

Nigeria and Benin established diplomatic relations on 12 September 1961. Benin enjoys stable relations with Nigeria, the main regional power. In fact, Benin is dependent on Nigeria for most of its exports. It is often asserted that Nigeria maintains exemplary relations with the Republic of Benin. An examination of the facts shows that the relations between the two states during the first decade of independence bordered first on neglect and later on misunderstandings owing to Benin's collaboration with the International Committee of the Red Cross in airlifting relief materials to the victims of the Nigerian civil war[117]. Given this, the subsequent decades were to witness an amelioration and a consolidation of the bilateral links between the two states. Benin, which before 1972 was assailed by bewildering political instability and has always been confronted by economic and financial crises, looked forward to exploiting the vast potential of the Nigerian

---

[117]*Nigeria-Benin relations: the joy and anguish of bilateralism // Leiden University catalogue.*

market. On its own part, Nigeria encouraged this bilateralism as a way of winning, exercising influence, and ensuring the security of its immediate threshold. However, the density of the unofficial cross-border transactions between the nationals of the two states undermines their official relations. Nigeria's low-key military cooperation as well as its nationalistic economic policy in the wake of diminished petroleum revenue underscore the limitations of this bilateralism.

In 1981, Nigeria and the Benin Republic created a Joint Border Commission to address issues such as border conflict, smuggling, irredentism, etc. The commission was charged with dealing with incursions by troops from the other side of the country. Following this development, a conference on Nigeria-Benin border cooperation was held in Lagos, where the issues of border demarcation, illegal immigration, and the harassment of people were addressed.

Meanwhile, Muhammadu Buhari closed Nigeria's land border with its Limitrophe neighbours in April 1984, despite all the mutual agreement reached for free movement of people and material in the region. However, this decision was believed to have paved the way for the effective implementation of the change in Nigerian currency. It was argued that the border closure was a response to the threat of smuggled goods from neighbouring countries entering Nigeria through their border, which had crippled the Nigerian domestic industries.

Nevertheless, Muhammadu Buhari's decision to close Nigeria's land borders with its immediate neighbours was vehemently condemned by the Economic Community of West African States (ECOWAS). It was regarded as a breach of the ECOWAS protocol on an open border and free movement of persons and goods across the subregion[118]. Asiwaju, (2003) stated that Nigeria's land borders were reopened immediately after Muhammadu Buhari's regime in 1986. However, the trend of open borders characterised Nigeria's foreign relations with its neighbours until the end of Buhari's administration.

The period of the border closure affected the relations between Nigeria and the affected countries, especially the relationship of the people living between the border communities that had lived together

---

[118] *Supplementary Protocol A/P.1/5/79 relating to Free Movement of Persons, Residence and Establishment. 1979.*

for several years[119]. Nevertheless, President Buhari's new agendas towards border cooperation are not a deviation from the previous agendas during his military era as head of state from 1983 to 1985 and later as president in a democratic regime from 2015 until the present. For emphasis, Muhammadu Buhari during his military regime, closed Nigeria's land border with its Limitrophe neighbours, despite all the mutual agreements reached for free movement of people and material in the region[120].

## Nigeria-Cameroon Relations

Bilateral relations between Nigeria and Cameroon since they attained independence in 1960 have been characterised by conflicts and cooperation driven by the perceived national interests of the political leadership at each point in time. The boundary dispute between Nigeria and the Cameroon Republic arising from their long, but ill-defined, border (1680 kilometres or 1050 miles) is of colonial origin (Osita, 2022).

However, it has remained a source of conflict in the direct bilateral relations between the two countries since their independence. In one form or another, the dispute has engaged the attention of almost all Nigerian governments since 1960. Many informed Nigerians believe that the Balewa government in the First Republic lost an opportunity to resolve the dispute to Nigeria's maximum satisfaction in 1960-1961. That opportunity, they claim, was lost because of a myopic and fratricidal conception of national interest in Nigeria's domestic politics. That loss continues to haunt Nigeria to date, particularly with respect to the maritime section, where its acclaimed vital security and strategic interests stand threatened, and also where Nigeria continues to suffer the humiliation of seeing the Cameroonian authorities administer a territory in the disputed area whose population is 90 percent Nigerian nationals.

---

[119] *President Buhari order for Nigeria land border closure // BBC News, 25 September 2019.*

[120] *Supplementary Protocol on the Code of Conduct for the Implementation of the Protocol on Free Movement of Persons, the Right of Residence and Establishment. 1985.*

Ironically, what was considered a national blunder in the immediate independence period was almost re-enacted in 1975, this time more consciously, when the Gowon administration signed the Maroua agreement with President Ahidjo's government in Cameroon, an agreement that effectively would have ceded the channel of the Calabar River and a portion of the Cross River estuary to Cameroon. As it turned out, the Maroua agreement is null and void in law as it was never ratified by Nigeria, leaving open the prospect of a new form of arrangement with the Cameroonians for solving the dispute in a mutually beneficial manner for both sides[121].

However, the dispute between Cameroon and Nigeria over the Bakassi Peninsula has assumed great prominence because of its richness in oil. It is important to note, however, that the case of Bakassi is only one element in the dispute that extends to the land boundary between Nigeria and Cameroon from the Lake Chad region to the coast. This long-standing dispute over the ownership of the Bakassi Peninsula, which was apparently laid to rest by the ruling of the International Court of Justice, provides an example of judicial arbitration at the international level. The ownership of the Bakassi Peninsula was a protracted dispute that involved several attempts by leaders and representatives of both countries to resolve it, although without success. Indeed, such has been the doggedness of both countries in their claims that they witnessed the eruption of violence on several occasions.

## Nigeria-Chad Relations

Nigeria and Chad have a history of bilateral relations dating from the pre-colonial era until the present. The determinants of Nigeria-Chad relations are not primarily based on the natural frontiers that exist between both states. They are shaped by the social forces of historical affinities in the people's culture, religion, and colonial history. The dynamics of contemporary Nigerian-Chad bilateral relations were systematically shaped by colonialism. While the French were in Chad, the British were in Nigeria to influence their foreign policy behaviour.

---

[121] *Analysis of Nigeria-Cameroon Relations // Project*

France and Britain laid the foundation for strong colonial ties between the colonised states of Chad and Nigeria.

Nigeria's relationship with Chad was not without its strains. Beginning in the late 1970s, clashes occurred around Lake Chad, where both countries hoped to exploit oil reserves. Both also sought to defuse these confrontations, first by establishing joint patrols and a commission to demarcate the boundary across the lake more clearly. Then, in the early 1980s, the low level of Lake Chad brought a series of tiny islands into view, leading to further disputes and disrupting long-standing informal trade networks.

Nigeria's own instability in the north, generated by rising Islamic fundamentalism also complicated this relationship. Thousands of casualties occurred as the result of violent clashes in Nigeria throughout the 1980s. Most religious violence was domestic in origin, but Nigerian police arrested a few Libyans, and Nigerian apprehension of Libyan infiltration through Chad intensified.

Nigeria's 1983 economic austerity campaign also produced strains with neighbouring states, including Chad. Nigeria expelled several hundred thousand foreign workers, mostly from its oil industry, which faced drastic cuts as a result of declining world oil prices. At least 30,000 of those expelled were Chadians.

Also, Nigeria faced a border dispute with Chad, and its government even contemplated military action against Chad. The Nigerian and Chadian dispute, which started during the second republic, was a complicated problem over control of islands on Lake Chad. It officially commenced when Chadian Army Chief – of –Staff Idriss Deby, led a force that invaded parts of Nigeria's Borno State. In spite of this, the Nigerian force led by Muhammadu Buhari was able to expel the Chadians and briefly invade Chadian territory[122]. Despite these strains, however, Nigerians had assisted in the halting process of achieving stability in Chad, and both nations reaffirmed their intention to maintain close ties.

---

[122] *Nigeria Interim Report. No. 24. February 29, 1984 //CSIS Africa Notes.*

## Nigeria-Niger Relations

Since independence in 1960, the two states have pursued close relations. Each side has based diplomatic relations on non-interference in the internal affairs of the other. Nigerian and Nigerian relations are based on a long-shared border and common cultural and historical interactions. The 1,500-kilometre-long (930-mile) border between Niger to the north and Nigeria to the south cuts through one of the more densely populated areas of both nations. Culturally, the centre and west of this border bisect the northern section of Hausa land, the home of the Hausa people. Before the turn of the 20th century, there was no formal border here, but the current line is roughly the northern reach of the 19th-century Sokoto Caliphate.

The expansion of French and British imperialism in the period 1890–1905 demarcated the line that would become the modern Nigeria–Niger border. During colonial rule, the French and English languages were implanted on each side of the border, along with cultural, educational, and political traditions. Rival French and British interests meant that during much of the colonial period, trade and relations across this border were dissuaded.

Nevertheless, the guiding principle of Nigeria's regional foreign policy was that of good neighbourliness and friendship. Nigeria's border with Niger provides an opportunity for both countries to promote and build on existing relations altered by colonialism and the creation of boundary lines separating the people into different territories, which is one of the legacies of colonialism on Africa that emanated from the resolution of the Berlin Conference of 1884/85[123]. (Vladimir, 2021), while reviewing issues related to Africa's regional identity and tradition, argues that the division of Africa into small sovereign states has helped to create a unique identity among peoples who became powerful symbols of national pride and interest.

However, the mixed relations between Nigeria and Niger have created suspicion and fear of Nigeria based on its military capacity, population, and economic resources. As Jackson (2017) pointed out, the border areas between Nigeria and Niger have served as a medium

---

[123] *Resolution of the Berlin Conference of 1884-1885.*

to foster its national interest through political, economic, and sociocultural relations among the people.

For clarity, Nigeria–Niger cooperation was established in 1971 to resolve various forms of challenges facing both countries, especially as it relates to the issues of borders and communities. For instance, the countries have organised several sessions of the Council of Ministers of the Joint Commission, which has conceived warehouses in Konni and Maradi (Niger Republic), border markets, and bilateral chamber of commerce[124].

**Promoting Border Cooperation.** It was in the national interest of Nigeria that Ibrahim Babangida reopened Nigeria's land borders with its Limitrophe neighbours in 1986, which were closed by Muhammadu Buhari, his predecessor, in April 1984. The Ibrahim Babangida administration sought a lasting solution to boundary issues with Nigeria's Limitrophe neighbours. This development led his administration to establish the National Boundary Commission (NBC) to resolve boundary challenges emanating from both internal and external boundaries with Nigeria's immediate neighbours[125].

It is crucial to note that the National Boundary Commission (NBC) has organised several trans-border cooperation workshops. Nigeria, through the National Boundary Commission, has engaged its neighbours —Niger, Chad, Cameroon, Equatorial Guinea, and the Republic of Benin—in activities that promote trans-border engagement, confidence-building, and peaceful co-existence. For example, the Nigeria-Niger trans-border cooperation workshop was held in 2002; the Nigeria-Benin Republic trans-border cooperation workshop was held in 1988; the Nigeria-Cameroon trans-border cooperation workshop was held in 1992; and the Nigeria-Equatorial Guinea trans-border cooperation workshop was held in 1992. Since this initiative started, the workshop has solved many boundary and border issues in Nigeria and other countries. For instance, the National Boundary Commission, under the leadership of Adamu Adaji has

---

[124]*Agreement of Understanding and Treaties Between Nigeria and other Countries. Office of the Secretary to the Government of the Federation, Nigeria.*
[125]*Ibid.*

helped to resolve the territorial issues between Taraba and Plateau state, as well as Abia and Akwa Ibom states, all situated in Nigeria. The Commission urged the various communities to cooperate and support the completion of seamless border demarcation between them[126].

In accordance with the National Boundary Commission's objectives of intellectual dialogue, the NBC has resolved several borders–related issues in a friendly atmosphere. According to Asiwaju (1993), the trans-border cooperation workshops serve as a laboratory where solutions to border conflicts and efforts to promote regional integration are deliberated upon in the interest of the region.

Furthermore, the idea of the trans-border cooperation workshops was conceived by the then Commissioner of International Boundaries in the National Boundary Commission (Asiwaju, 1993). According to him, the entire project is aimed at establishing a border-specific bilateral cooperative policy and practice between Nigeria and each of the five adjacent countries.

For instance, the National Boundary Commission has held several conferences and workshops on trans-border cooperation between Nigeria and its immediate neighbours. Following this, a workshop was held in 1988 in the ancient town of Badagry, titled the Nigeria-Benin Trans-border Cooperation Workshop. Another workshop was held in Kano between Nigeria and Niger in 1989. Yola hosted the Trans-Border Cooperation Workshop between Nigeria and Cameroon in 1992. In 1992, the Nigeria–Equatorial Guinea Trans-border Cooperation Workshop was held in Calabar. The Nigeria–Niger Trans-border Cooperation Workshop of 2002 took place in Sokoto (Asiwaju, 1993).

Over the years, border issues have confronted Nigeria and its neighbours, and these workshops have provided a platform to discuss them. An array of issues affecting border communities between Nigeria and its adjacent countries are discussed during the workshops to establish areas of cooperation between Nigeria and its neighbours.

It was evident from the trans-border cooperation workshops held that scholars and professional bodies, as well as traditional rulers from

---

[126] *NBC urges Plateau, Taraba communities to cooperate for smooth border demarcation // The Guardian, February 20, 2021.*

both sides of the international border, had presented their cases on an array of topical issues. According to Asiwaju et al. (1992), the workshops look at issues in local administration, culture, the border economy, legal issues, and conclude with conclusions, delimitation questions on border security, and recommendations. The trans-border cooperation workshop has contributed to border cooperation in the areas of political and socio-economic development between Nigeria and its immediate neighbours in the interest of the sub-region[127].

The success of trans-border cooperation workshops through the National Boundary Commission influenced similar programmes in West Africa. In 1999, the Malian government influenced by the Nigerian model and established the National Borders Directorate, which promoted the policy concept of the border country or cross border area in 2002. In the same vein, the Economic Community of West African States launched its version of the programme, titled ECOWAS Cross – Border Initiatives Programme (CIP) in 2005 – 2006[128]. However, the commission focuses on local cross-border cooperation and has designed several means for promoting the cross-border concept and ensuring its implementation in the years to come. The irredentism and boundary disputes arising from the manner in which the West African states were partitioned in Berlin, Germany, in 1884/85[129] were mitigated by the Ibrahim Babangida administration in 1987 through the establishment of the National Boundary Commission, which then promoted border cooperation between Nigeria and its immediate neighbours (Ahmad, 2015).

Notwithstanding, President Muhammadu Buhari in August 2019 ordered the closure of Nigeria's land borders, claiming that the illegal smuggling activities have hindered the economic development of Nigeria. According to him, Nigeria can only develop and enhance its

---

[127] *The Nigeria – Benin Transborder Cooperation: proceeding of the Bilateral Workshop at the Administrative Staff College of Badagry, Nigeria. May 9-13, 1988.*
[128] *The ECOWAS Cross-Border Initiatives Programme. Sahel West Africa Club Secretariat.*
[129] *Resolution of the Berlin Conference of 1884-1885.*

economic infrastructure when there is no more illegal smuggling of goods and services from neighbouring states[130].

**Nigeria and the formation of ECOWAS.** It is a fact of history that Nigeria played a prominent role in the formation of the Economic Community of West African States (ECOWAS) in 1975[131]. The original intention of the community emanates from Article 2 of the Treaty of Lagos, which was aimed to promote, regulate, and develop all fields of economic activities in order to improve the living standard, maintain economic stability, and promote close relations between ECOWAS member states (Jenkins, 2008). Before the establishment of the Economic Community of West African States in 1975, individual state handled the political, economic, and security problems in the West African region. However, collective efforts towards economic challenges gained traction in West Africa after the Nigeria–Biafra civil war in 1970. Out of enlightened self-interest, Nigeria's former Head-of-State, General Yakubu Gowon (retired), liaised with the late Togolese President, Gnassingbe Eyadema, to establish a regional economic organisation ECOWAS, to concertedly manage the economic and political challenges in the West African region.

According to Sinclair (1983), Nigeria's participation in West African economic integration attracts political and economic stability in its subregion. He believed that Nigeria's role in the late 1960s and 1970s was to woo other West African states, to which it belongs, into a regional economic agreement for harmonisation of the economic policies of newly independent African states, trade liberalisation, and the joint coordination of economic development. Nwalie (2020), while re-examining the Nigerian political leadership strategy in West Africa, argued that Nigeria's involvement in the creation of ECOWAS is to maintain its regional hegemonic status.

Notwithstanding, ECOWAS, at its initial stage, posits an economic organisation that was bestowed with the task of ending economic instabilities in the region. However, the organisation steadily adapts to prevailing security problems within the subregion on the grounds that

---

[130] *President Buhari order for Nigeria land border closure. // BBC News, 25 September 2019.*
[131] *The Lagos Treaty of 1975.*

the economy can only excel in a conducive atmosphere of nonviolence.

In line with this judgment, ECOWAS was obliged to evolve into an organisation bearing the onerous burden of resolving an accumulated security problem in the subregion. Nevertheless, ECOWAS has since committed itself, through the Protocols on peaceful intervention in conflict areas, to providing security to states in distress and crises[132].

According to Katharina (2017), the principles and norms established by the ECOWAS for a peacekeeping mission have served as a model for African organisations in considering regional peace enforcement operations. However, she argued that ECOWAS has always been at the forefront of pushing liberal interpretations of sovereignty, especially as it relates to the possibility of collective intervention during times of conflict.

Another emphasis in creating the Economic Community of West African States was the liberalisation of inter-community trade and related forms of cooperation, such as regional economic communities that were fully supported by ECOWAS member states[133]. Although other areas of ECOWAS activities considered are measures to facilitate the free flow of people, through the introduction of visa–free travel for citizens of West African countries within the region and recognition of people's right to reside and settle in any country of the region[134].

To buttress this, Olatunde (1980), argued that Nigeria's role in ECOWAS integration processes is another effort to institutionalise the concept of pan–Africanism. He claimed that Nigeria's interest is divided into two variables; first variables explain Nigeria's role in the initiation and maintenance of ECOWAS, giving insight into the future behaviour of the organisation, and the second variables elaborate on Nigeria's interest in African diplomacy as relates to the concept of Pan–Africanism. Thus, Nigeria's role in the formation of ECOWAS was confirmed by its national interests and foreign policy pursuits,

---

[132] *ECOWAS Protocol Relating to the Mechanism for Conflict Prevention, Mechanism, Management, Resolution, Peacekeeping and Security, 1999.*
[133] *Treaty Establishing the African Economic Community of 1991.*
[134] *Supplementary Protocol on the Code of Conduct for the Implementation of the Protocol on Free Movement of Persons, the Right of Residence and Establishment. 1985.*

which were designed to promote regional integration and cooperation within West Africa. Thus, Nigeria has also played an important role in mitigating the political and economic instabilities in its subregion.

**Afrocentric Doctrine.** Nigeria's foreign policy during the formative years of ECOWAS was defined by the prevailing circumstances in the region that allowed the kind of foreign policy that was premeditated to respond to the frequent political instabilities across the region because of incessant military coups, religious intolerance, a lack of social and economic development, and the supremacy struggle between Anglophone and Francophone countries in the region due to their historical experience (Nwalie, 2020). However, Nigeria's foreign policy has prioritised its support for the Economic Community of West African States in realising its developmental and security goals. According to Olonisakin (2004), the ECOWAS initiatives have prevented West African countries from resorting to violence through political and diplomatic means.

More importantly, Nigeria's Afrocentric foreign policy towards ECOWAS serves as an exemplar of its broader foreign policy concept; in this context, Nigeria sought to support ECOWAS for its foreign policy-related goals. To amplify this, Gill (1989) claimed that most countries promote multilateral relations to ensure a stable political and economic climate in the global space, which will secure the smooth running of goods and services across borders. He believed Nigeria's contribution to ECOWAS and other regional organisations conformed to its multilateral diplomacy.

However, Nigeria has diverse views on why ECOWAS is important to its foreign policy pursuits. Among the phenomena is the centrality of three specific challenges that lie at the heart of Nigeria's foreign policy: its need to protect national security and power, on the one hand, and to act as a regional power, in other words, as an African leader, on the other hand; the second phenomenon is Nigeria's quest to redefine itself within the transforming regional and global orders in West Africa and beyond; and lastly, Nigeria's interpreted utility of ECOWAS is that Nigeria hopes that the organisation will help to project a well-coordinated and cohesive policy in pursuing its interests in the rest of the subregion (Obi, 2008).

Meanwhile, the activities of non-state transnational actors at the domestic level also contribute to Nigeria's foreign policy successes towards ECOWAS and its member states. According to Adebajo et al. (2008), Nigeria remains West Africa's unarguable hegemon and pivotal state, though its external projection in ECOWAS and beyond is forecast upon a weak domestic base, resulting in an inefficient foreign policy towards its subregion and beyond. While Omo–Ogbebor (2017), Nigeria's funding for the 15 member bodies stood at three to six times what other nations contributed. That ratio rose recently to over 60 percent of ECOWAS's total revenues with the introduction of community levies, according to data showing annual state-wide contributions.

**Nigeria's leadership.** Nigeria's leadership role in ECOWAS could be determined by its financial contribution to ECOWAS and its member states (Nwalie et al., 2022). Nigeria's huge contribution to ECOWAS can be traced to the ECOWAS Community Levy Agreement, which was adopted in 1996 by the Authority of Heads of State as the major funding for ECOWAS after the initial contribution regime seemed ineffective. The Community Levy Protocol took effect in 2003, when all member states started its application. For emphasis, the protocol stipulates that the taxable base shall be all goods originating from third countries (non-ECOWAS countries) imported into the community.

Moreover, Nigeria paid more than $1,177 billion to the Economic Community of West African States (ECOWAS) as its Community Levy contribution in the last 16 years because of the tax on imported goods. Nigeria's payment represents 40.42 per cent of the total payment of $2,913,088,908 made by all 15 member states and is higher than the payments made by 12 other countries put together, except Ghana and Cote d'Ivoire. Ghana paid about $508,577 million, Cote d'Ivoire $347,262 million, and Benin, Burkina Faso, Cape Verde, Guinea, Guinea-Bissau, Gambia, Liberia, Mali, Niger, Senegal, Sierra Leone, and Togo paid a total of $879,711 million[135].

It is crucial to note that many countries have yet to comply with the payment of their community levy. Furthermore, the community

---

[135] *Nigeria contributed $1.17bn to ECOWAS in 16 years // Premium Times July 29, 2020.*

levy data showed that many countries were yet to pay the total sum from their community levy assessments. Based on the assessment, if all countries had paid in full, the sub-regional body would have gotten more than $3,710 billion as against the $2,913 billion paid, leaving a deficit of $797,215 million. Based on this assessment, Nigeria had paid 64 per cent of its payments, leaving an outstanding balance of 36 per cent.

Nigeria's foreign policy approach towards the ECOWAS regional agenda is based on the Afrocentric foreign policy doctrine, which was directed at its West African neighbours because Nigeria sees the West African region as an integral part of its foreign policy. Nigerian foreign policy towards the ECOWAS regional agenda is guided by its 1999 constitution, which outlines the objectives of its foreign policy direction. In Chapter II, Section 19 of the Federal Republic of Nigeria as amended, projects a dynamic foreign policy for Nigeria through the promotion of economic development, integration and unity, peace, and security in West Africa, Africa, and the world.

Since 1999, the Nigerian foreign policy approach towards ECOWAS has witnessed a proactive response. Nigeria, under President Olusegun Obasanjo's administration, reinforced the country's position as Africa's regional hegemony. For instance, the President Olusegun Obasanjo administration advocated four broad issue areas that Africa must address to attract lasting peace and security. These include redirecting the mind, redefining sovereignty, a redefinition of security, and institutionalisation democracy (Obasanjo, 1999)[136].

For emphasis, on February 26, 2012, Nigeria's former President Olusegun Obasanjo was charged with the responsibility to engage all political stakeholders in Senegal, where protests by opposition parties over the presidential term dispute resulted in the loss of lives and destruction of property[137]. In this light, President Goodluck Jonathan also appointed by ECOWAS in 2015 as a special envoy to head its mediation mission in Mali. Meanwhile, President Goodluck Jonathan

---

136 *Obasanjo O. (1999). Who is Obasanjo. View Article: DOI: http://olusegunobasanjo.org/hiscareer.php. (accessed on: 09.06.2021).*

137 *Obasanjo O. Lead joint AU-ECOWAS mission to Senegal // Reliefweb, February 19, 2012.*

facilitated dialogue with all Malian parties, including President Ibrahim Boubacar Keita, opposition leaders, religious organisations and civil society, which resulted in the quelling of the socio-political unrest in the country.

Apparently, Nigeria has exhibited its leadership role through various ECOWAS protocols in the peaceful resolution of the political crises in Sierra Leone, Liberia, and Togo. Nigeria equally gets involved while playing the lead role in the Mano River dispute between Liberia, Guinea, and Sierra Leone, thus bringing an end to the sequence of hostility prevalent within the region. Finally, the Nigerian foreign policy towards ECOWAS regional initiatives has directly or indirectly contributed to the growth of the organisation and the development of the region at large, especially in spheres of the economic scheme, security formation, and promotion of political stability through democracy and good governance. Thus, Nigerian engagement in ECOWAS activities is carried out through bilateral and multilateral diplomacy to meet the expectations of the international community as a regional leader.

The 40th Ordinary Session of the Authority of ECOWAS Heads of State and Government appointed former Nigerian President, President Olusegun Obasanjo, and President Goodluck Jonathan as ECOWAS conflict resolution chairperson and special envoy to head its mediation mission in Senegal and Mali, respectively, and from 1990 to 1999, Nigerian military commander Joshua Dogonyaro and eight other Nigerian military commanders[138]spearheaded the ECOMOG troops to Liberia, which in turn produced the expected result as required by the ECOWAS (Abegunrin, 2003).

Nigeria's foreign policy concept towards ECOWAS and its member states is based on the Afrocentric foreign policy doctrine, which is the premise of its foreign policy direction after attaining

---

[138]*The eight other Nigerian military commanders were Maj-Gen. Rufus Kupolati, Field Commander. February 1991 – Sept. 1991; Maj-Gen. Ishaya Baku, Field Commander. Sept. 1991- October 1992; Maj-Gen. Tunji Olurin, Field Commander. October 1992 - October 1993; Maj-Gen. John Shagaya, Field Commander. Oct. 1993 - December 1993; Maj-Gen. John Mark Inienger, Field Commander. December 1993 - August 1996; Maj-Gen. Victor Malu, Force Commander. August 1996 - January 1998; Maj-Gen. Timothy Shelpidi, Force Commander. January 1998 - March 1999; Maj-Gen. Felix Mujakperuo, Force Commander. 1999.*

independence to support the cause of African countries struggling for independence in the 1960s. The Afrocentric foreign policy doctrine was efficient at the domestic level as it was directed at its West African neighbours because Nigeria sees the West African region as its natural territory.

## 2.4 Nigeria and Multilateral Institutions in West Africa

Since independence, Nigeria's foreign policy has been characterised by a focus on Africa and, by extension, West African institutions. Nigeria's relations with the Lake Chad Basin Commission and Gulf of Guinea Commission are necessitated as a result of the following goals: to exercise hegemonic influence in the region; to regulate and control utilisation of the water and other natural resources in the basin; to uphold African unity and independence; and to examine complaints and promote settlement of disputes, with a view to promoting regional economic cooperation and development. Nigeria, according to Akinkugbe (2013), has a highly respected profile in Africa that is considered emulating various African issues, and that profile has largely been that of an active member of the international community, a central player in subregional and African affairs

In line with this judgment, Nigeria participates in the activities of the Lake Chad Basin Commission[139] and the Gulf of Guinea Commission. Nigeria has enjoyed generally good relations with the abovementioned institutions in several dimensions. Nigeria's quest to cooperate, regulate, and control the utilisation of water and other natural resources in its subregion has necessitated the establishment of the Lake Chad Basin Commission. The commission was established by a convention and statute signed on 22 May 1964, by Cameroon, Chad, Niger, Nigeria, and later by the Central African Republic, Algeria, Libya, and Sudan[140].The goals and objectives of the commission are to regulate and control the utilisation of water and other natural resources

---

[139] *The N' Djamena Chad of 1964. Agreement Establishing the Lake Chad Basin Commission. 1964.*
[140] *Lake Chad Basin Commission.*

in the basin[141]; to examine complaints and promote the settlement of disputes; to promote regional cooperation; and to initiate, promote, and coordinate natural resource development projects and research within the basin area.

The Lake Chad Basin Commission was also instituted in pursuance of achieving the following mandate: (1) to sustainably and equitably manage the Lake Chad and other shared water resources of the Lake Chad Basin; (2) to promote regional integration, peace, and security across the basin; and (3) to preserve the ecosystems of the Lake Chad Conventional Basin.

Of all these concerns, Ogilvie (2010) argued that the Nigerian government has considered collaborative measures with other West African countries as the only panacea to address the tension in the Lake Chad region. For instance, on the issues of national security threats in Lake Chad, collaborative measures by Nigeria and its neighbours to curb trans-border crimes and strengthen subregional security were considered during the signing of the Transborder Security Cooperation Agreement with Cameroon in 2012[142] and the establishment of the Multi-National Joint Task Force (MNJTF) under the aegis of the Lake Chad Basin Commission, which comprises Nigeria, Niger, Cameroon and Chad for effective joint border patrols[143].

In the same light, Nigerian President Muhammadu Buhari, during the United Nations General Assembly Plenary in 2018, advocated for global action on the Lake Chad crisis. According to President Muhammadu Buhari, illegal immigration is not just a consequence of conflict but also of the impacts of climate change and a lack of opportunities. The president emphasised the need for better cooperation over water, which constitutes a vital lifeline for people and nature in this semiarid region of West and Central Africa[144]. Climate

---

[141]*Convention and statutes relating to the development of the Chad basin. Signed at Fort Lamy, on 22 May, 1964.*
[142]*Agreement on Transborder Security Cooperation. Cameroon, Nigeria Agree to Bolster Cooperation against Transborder Terrorism. 2012.*
[143]*Ministry of Foreign Affairs, Abuja, Nigeria and Africa Relations.*
[144] *Report of the UNGA transcript. The Chad Basin, Lifeline for People Nature and Peace. 2019.*

change, according to Oguntade (2012), has the potential to reduce water availability in West Africa.

Similarly, President Muhammadu Buhari, on May 25, 2021, at the opening of the Extraordinary Summit of Heads of State and Government of the Lake Chad Basin Commission (LCBC), was summoned to deliberate on the recent happenings in Chad after President Idris Deby Itno died on the frontlines while defending the territorial integrity of his country. President Muhammadu Buhari declared Nigeria ready to support the fight against insurgency in the Lake Chad region; he urged all leaders within the Lake Chad region and international development partners to rise to the need for peace and stability to be restored in the region[145].

Furthermore, the challenges being faced by African states in Lake Chad have contributed to the underdevelopment of the region and required a joint effort of countries in the lake and the support of the international community to avert the destabilisation of many African states located in the region. As Nigeria's national interest is supreme and fundamental in its relations with the outside world, the issue of Africa, which has remained a cornerstone of its foreign policy,[146] has become a basis for its interest in the lake region, but since it could not do it alone, successive administrations in Nigeria, including the present, have viewed the approach of seeking a collaborative effort of the international community with the support of countries located in the lake region to handle those challenges plaguing the West African region.

Following the 1999 inauguration of a civilian president, the Nigerian-Gulf of Guinea country's cooperation began to improve in the areas of regional economic cooperation and development.

In line with this judgment, President Olusegun Obasanjo, in conjunction with other African presidents residing in the Gulf of Guinea, signed a treaty for the establishment of the Gulf of Guinea Commission on 3 July 2001[147]. The treaty is targeted to develop close and multifaceted cooperation among member states and to establish a

---

[145] *President Muhammadu Buhari Declaration on Lake Chad Region // Xinhua News Agency, May 25, 2021.*
[146] *Ministry of Foreign Affairs, Abuja, Nigeria and Africa Relations.*
[147] *The Libreville Gabon of 2001. Treaty of Establishing Gulf of Guinea Commission.*

relationship on the basis of mutual understanding, good neighbourliness and strong bonds of friendship. This, among other factors, has been promoting and protecting the integrity and welfare of Nigeria and its neighbours within the context of unity and development (Ogunnubi, 2018). All of this was in tandem and in consonance with Nigeria's first prime minister's ideas to commensurate with Nigeria's name and status as a 'messiah' of the continent.

Again, the concept of good neighbourliness was given more credible and emphatic attention when Jaja Anucha Wachuku, the Nigerian first Minister of Foreign Affairs, stated that any Nigeria's foreign policy that does not connote the interest of the common man on the continent of Africa is unrealistic. According to him, charity begins at home; thus, the dividend of Nigeria's foreign policy should be seen in the affairs of the people.

The emphasis on Nigeria's national interest in the Gulf of Guinea is in accordance with its foreign policy pursuits. Nigeria is a member of the Economic Community of West African States (ECOWAS), while a sizeable number of countries in the Gulf of Guinea are also members of the Economic Community of West African States. However, the Regional Maritime Security of Central Africa (CRESMAC) for the Economic Community of Central African States (ECCAS) is based in Pointe Norie, Republic of Congo, while the Regional Centre for Maritime Security of West Africa (CRESMAO) is based in Cote d'Ivoire. The duo was established in February 2015[148].

Having these two regional maritime securities in place and for effective coordination was the establishment of the Inter-Regional Coordination Centre in Yaounde, Cameroon, which was part of the Maritime Security Architecture of West and Central Africa, to fill the gap of coordination between the three regions in the war against criminal activities in the maritime domain of the Gulf of Guinea Region[149].

---

[148] *Official document of the Ministry of Foreign Affairs on the Gulf of Guinea Commission, African Sub-Regional Organizations (ASROD) Division, 14th September, 2018.*
[149] *Ibid*

Since Nigeria, according to Ujara (2014), is regarded as the giant of Africa in terms of population, human resources, and natural resources put together, and in its national interest, the country is expected to take a leading role in solving the various problems confronting the Gulf of Guinea region and even beyond.

According to George (2010), the policy document prepared by the Ministry of Foreign Affairs of Nigeria showed the process of establishing the Gulf of Guinea Commission; nevertheless, it was contemplated that when the Commission took off, it would be a multilateral body devoted to cooperation among the countries that share the geographical formation known as the Gulf of Guinea and would equally serve as a platform for promoting the interests of the constituent states in the areas of the environment, politics, security, and economy.

Since the issue of the Gulf of Guinea Commission is vital to some African states that are members of the commission, they have adopted an approach of informing major powers of its activities. To buttress this, Gromoglasova (2016) argued that Africa and the world are witnessing a new stage in the war on terror, which has hindered economic development in most developing countries, especially West African countries, for example, Boko Haram activities. She claimed that the GGC approach to reaffirming the responsibility of the state for suppressing terrorist groups operating from within its territory seems to have become more acceptable, and if the state cannot suppress terrorist activity, it should accept counter–terrorist interventions on its territory. Since maritime security in the Gulf of Guinea region is beyond African countries, the Commission always consults with the US and other Western countries interested in the activities of the Commission for their possible assistance in getting rid of criminals and developing the region.

President Muhammadu Buhari emerged as the Chairman of the Gulf of Guinea Commission on 23 November 2017[150]. In his acceptance speech, the President declared Nigeria's readiness and position to curtail the socio-economic and security challenges

---

[150] *Statement by Muhammadu Buhari as the Chairman of Gulf of Guinea Commission // Independent, November 27, 2017.*

bedevilling the Gulf of Guinea. President Muhammadu Buhari claims in his submission that the members would only achieve the set goals and objectives of the commission through a collective measure.

Again, President Muhammadu Buhari, on July 7, 2021, in a virtual audience with the Executive Secretary of the Commission, Florentina Ukonga, reiterated Nigerian interest in fortifying the Gulf Guinea Commission to enable the commission to perform the roles for which it was set up[151].

In line with this development, Khudaykulova (2016) claimed that the approach and method used in fighting security challenges in developing countries, particularly African countries such as Nigeria, Chad, Cameroon, etc are different from the Western approach. She believed that most of the unrest and security threats in African states are internally generated, such as the issue of Boko Haram in Nigeria, which has caused much menace in the West African subregion.

Meanwhile, the security situation in the West African subregion was not the only reason Nigeria showed much interest in West African institutions; other factors were put together that would harness the economic development of the region in the interest of the continent.

Finally, Nigeria's foreign policy at the subregional level is characterised by both economic and political imperatives, which are conducted on two levels: bilateral and multilateral relations. It is on this premise that both the successive and present administrations in Nigeria have taken the development of their subregion as a priority. However, the President Muhammadu Buhari administration needs to open the door to new possibilities for re-engaging all the subregional institutions and moving claims to leadership at the subregional level to actualise the goals and objectives of these institutions. This would require a radical rethinking of Nigeria's foreign policy, including a major transformation of its decision-making and implementation apparatus. It also means opening up the policy space to innovative knowledge-based strategies and ideas and feeding these into a coordinated and impactful manner in projecting Nigeria's interests and influence into its subregion and the continent of Africa.

---

[151] *President Muhammadu Buhari Interview with the Executive Secretary of the GGC, Florentina Ukonga // Premium Times, July 7, 2021.*

**Nigeria's in ECOWAS.** Nigeria's foreign policy objectives are aimed at rapprochement and active cooperation with neighbouring countries and regional organisations, specifically the Economic Community of West African States (ECOWAS), in the interest of the continent. However, the conception of regional integration that created the Economic Community of West African States (ECOWAS) in 1975 has provided an opportunity for Nigeria to exert its hegemonic influence in the West African region.

However, the path of Nigeria's engagement with the organisation has been a mix of hits and misses. According to Warner (2016), Nigeria has not fully actualised its leadership role, despite all the natural resources and power it possesses, as well as its institutional architecture that projects a vibrant foreign policy towards ECOWAS. However, he believed that the gap between the potential represented by Nigeria's natural resources and its performance as a regional leader poses a conundrum in Nigeria's foreign policy.

The main reason for Nigeria's foreign policy towards ECOWAS is that Nigeria sees the organisation as being an integral part of its national security and territorial integrity. This could be traced to the declaration made by Prime Minister Tafawa Balewa in his inaugural speech on 7 October 1960, at the Plenary of the 15th Regular Session of the United Nations General Assembly, exactly six days after Nigeria gained independence and became the 99th member of the organisation declared that Nigeria hoped to work with all African countries for the progress of Africa and to assist in bringing all African territories to a state of responsible independence and help in finding a lasting solution to the problem affecting Nigeria's immediate neighbors. Subsequently, Nigeria's political and economic policies towards ECOWAS were in connection with the objectives of Pan-Africanism and Nigeria's national interest, which are rooted in the nationalist struggle and the immediate post-independence period. Nevertheless, Nigeria's leaders have always seen the country's natural resources and its demographics as the basis for aspiring to continental leadership.

More importantly, Nigeria's status as a West African powerhouse has made it more logical that the country aspires to a leadership position and still regards ECOWAS as the arena for ventilating its hegemonic ambition in Africa. Nigeria's attributes to its subregion place the country in a position of influence and leadership, which in a null shell exposes the country to a vulnerability position where the quest for certain domestic constituencies and threats from within its immediate neighbours became uncertain.

To amplify this, Nolte (2010), in his comparison of regional powers, identifies certain criteria that need to be met to assume a leadership position, which are as follows: the domestic issues of such a state should allow it to play a stabilising and leading role in the region; such a state should make known its willingness and capacity to assume the role of a regional leader, stabiliser, and, of course, if not peacekeeper, at least peacemaker; and lastly, it should be acceptable to its neighbours, the members of the security complex in which it operates as a leader responsible for regional security. Nevertheless, the offer of leadership and service delivery by Nigeria has spread across all West African regions.

Nigeria's hegemonic position in West Africa can also be traced prior to the imposition of colonial borders. According to Adetula (2015), Nigerians in recent times had evolved long–standing historical, political, and economic relations with people from across West Africa before African territories were divided by European powers in the name of colonisation.

Nigeria's foreign policy towards ECOWAS activities under the military regime places more emphasis on the security aspect than economic advancement, which was the primary reason the organisation was created. However, the role Nigeria played in ECOWAS would help to harmonise trade and investment practices for ECOWAS member countries[152].

Finally, the constant changing of governments through the unconstitutional process was prevalent among ECOWAS members, thereby worsening the political and security situation in the region. This development was the reason political stability and security matters came to dominate the activities of ECOWAS in the 1980s and 1990s instead of economic integration, which was the primary reason why ECOWAS was formed. In addition, ECOWAS was created during the oil boom period in the world, which provided Nigeria with huge oil revenue to attend to the myriad of problems that confronted the

---

[152] *The Lagos Treaty of 1975.*

region and sustained the survival of ECOWAS during the turbulent years (Kostyunina, 2016).

**Nigerian Democratic Transition.** Since Nigeria transitioned to a democratic regime in 1999, following decades of military rule that have breached several aspects of Nigeria's foreign policy, President Olusegun Obasanjo took upon himself the mandate to restore the Nigerian lost image towards ECOWAS and its member states. In his inaugural speech, President Olusegun Obasanjo stresses the need for Nigeria to stay active at the central stage of regional and continental affairs. He declared that his administration would pursue a dynamic foreign policy aimed at developing friendly relations with all countries and would continue to play a constructive role in the activities of ECOWAS. He made it known that his administration is determined to fully restore Nigeria to its former prestigious position in the community of nations[153].

During Olusegun Obasanjo's tenure as President of Nigeria, Nigeria's foreign policy approach towards ECOWAS was an active response, which in turn strengthened the country's position as Africa's regional power. On this basis, Africa continued to attract the attention of Nigeria's foreign policy, with particular emphasis on advancing the ECOWAS regional agenda, development, peace, and security[154].

For emphasis, Nigeria's foreign policy towards the ECOWAS regional agenda is guided by its 1999 constitution, which outlines the objectives of its foreign policy direction. Chapter II, Section 19, of the Constitution of the Federal Republic of Nigeria 1999, as amended. Projects a dynamic foreign policy for Nigeria through the promotion of economic development, integration and unity, peace, and security in West Africa, Africa, and the world.

President Olusegun Obasanjo's administration contributed hugely to the restoration of peace in West Africa, especially in Sierra Leone

---

[153] *Inaugural Speech of President Olusegun Obasanjo, 29 May 1999, Federal Ministry of Information, Abuja.; Lt. Gen. Olusegun Obasanjo. Nigeria First" in Call to Duty: A Collection of Speeches // Federal Ministry of Information, Lagos. 1978, p. 33.*

[154] *Obasanjo Speaks on Nigerian Troops in Sierra Leone // Pan African News Agency, 2 March, 1999.*

and Liberia, despite Nigeria's low economic status, which cannot provide the needed resources for any large–scale regional peacekeeping efforts as of then.

However, after the reign of President Olusegun Obasanjo in 2007, his successors, President Musa Yar'Adua (2007–2010), President Goodluck Jonathan (2010–2015) and President Muhammadu Buhari, followed suit in pursuing a relatively low-key foreign policy. President Musa Yar'Adua's administration maintained the citizen diplomacy that was introduced by President Olusegun Obasanjo's administration, which sought to emphasise a people-centred approach to foreign policy[155].

Notwithstanding, the main objective of President Musa Yar'Adua's administration was to lift Nigeria's economy to become one of the 20 largest economies in the world by 2020. The agenda has been properly conceptualised and comprehensively articulated; thus, the implementation strategies were adequately laid out to ensure the realisation of ECOWAS Vision 2020, which Nigerians embraced with all their seriousness[156].

However, the controversy surrounding the 2007 general elections, internal challenges posed by the rising insurgency in the Niger Delta region, the escalation of insurgent violence by the extremist Boko Haram activities in the northeast (Walter Gam, 2013), President Musa Yar'Adua's poor state of health, and many other factors adversely affected Nigeria's foreign policy towards ECOWAS. To buttress this, Adeniyi (2011) says Nigeria missed out in the high-ranking international meetings, lost many positions in multilateral organisations, forsook obligations, and found itself in a situation where many of its allies started wondering what had gone wrong with Nigeria.

Meanwhile, President Musa Yar'Adua's administration used citizen diplomacy as an instrument to protect and cater for the welfare of Nigerian citizens and to promote the integrity of Nigerian institutions. In other words, the affairs of the regional organisations became secondary to his administration. Nigeria's foreign policy towards

---

[155] *Yar'Adua,U.M. Inauguration Speech of President, Nigerian Federal Ministry of Information &Communications,Vision 2020, Abuja, Aso Rock, 29 May 2007.*
[156] *Yar'Adua,U.M.Inauguration Speech of President, Nigerian Federal Ministry of Information & Communications,Vision 2020, Abuja, Aso Rock, 29 May 2007.*

ECOWAS during President Goodluck Jonathan's administration was fully in support of regional peace and security. This could be seen after President Goodluck Jonathan conceded defeat to Muhammadu Buhari in the keenly contested Nigerian 2015 elections. ECOWAS leaders applauded him at the summit of heads of state, which was held on 10 October, 2015[157].

The shift in Nigeria's foreign policy towards ECOWAS portrays huge spending on aid, extensive peace intervention, and support operations to contribute ideas on institutional reform for deepening democratic norms, regional peace and security, and cooperation in addressing transnational threats, which has both domestic and regional constraints on Nigeria's influence and aspirations to leadership. All these efforts made (Denisova, 2015) examine various ECOWAS initiatives and the problems member states encountered in their peacekeeping activities.

Although it could be argued that Nigeria's status as a regional power and a key player in ECOWAS has been diminishing over time due to domestic and regional security challenges, which have affected the economic development of the region (Ioannis, 2010), according to Irish (2014), President Goodluck Jonathan, in a bid to consolidate Nigeria's foreign policy, decided to reach out to Nigeria's neighbours: Chad, Cameroon, Niger, and Benin, at a meeting held in France to form a united front against Boko Haram insurgents.

Denisova (2016) argued that the high level of insecurity after the Nigerian general election in 2011, which conceived the Boko Haram insurgency, is associated with religious beliefs. She believes that the activities of the insurgents have continuously hindered the economic development of the Nigerian state and its subregion. However, President Goodluck Jonathan's administration was fully in support of ECOWAS zero tolerance for the unconstitutional and undemocratic change of government, despite the modifications to its foreign policy objectives[158].

---

[157] *Accra Summit to Review Regional Political, Security Situation. 2015. ECOWAS heads of state welcome the West African region's enormous progress.; ECOWAS Chairman congratulates President Jonathan, General Buhari. 2015.*

[158] *Inaugural Speech of President Goodluck Ebele Jonathan on 29 May 2011, Federal Ministry of Information, Abuja, Nigeria.*

Moreover, the emergence of Muhammadu Buhari as Nigeria's president on May 29, 2015, provided new leadership at the helm of Nigeria's foreign policy. Having won the election based on promises to tackle insecurity and fight against corruption and economic instability. President Muhammadu Buhari believes that his administration cannot tackle the problems alone without the concerted efforts of multilateral institutions. To support this notion of multilateralism Abolade (2005) believes it is one of the basic principles of Nigeria's foreign policy, in which the country has never reneged in its dealings with the outside world, especially the ECOWAS and its member states.

Nigeria's foreign policy towards the ECOWAS regional agenda under President Buhari's administration is somewhat a reverse; emphasis is placed on internal issues rather than getting too involved with external matters that will drill the country's lean resources[159]. Although Nigeria's foreign policy towards the ECOWAS regional security arrangement is not compromised, its continued support for ECOWAS's stand on unconstitutional change of government is unwavering, as demonstrated during the Burkina Faso and Gambian political crises.

Meanwhile, President Muhammadu Buhari, after his inauguration in 2015, embarked on shuttle diplomacy, visiting Nigeria's immediate neighbours, Chad, Niger, Cameroon, and Benin, to seek ways of quelling the Boko Haram insurgent operation in northeast Nigeria. (Oyeniyi, 2010), in his submission on terrorism in Nigeria, claimed that various groups in Nigeria agitate for the political, ethnic, and religious interests of their people; consequently, their activities over the years have affected the economic development of the country.

Moreover, Nigeria's foreign policy towards ECOWAS under President Muhammadu Buhari's administration is passing through a transformation period with no specific agenda except the old-age Afrocentric slogan, which has dominated its foreign policy formulations since its independence.

Finally, he claimed that President Muhammadu Buhari's approach towards ECOWAS and its member states conformed with his electoral

---

[159] *Inaugural Speech of President Muhammadu Buhari on 29 May 2015, Permanent Mission of Nigeria to the United Nations*

campaign promises to quell every manner of insurgencies in the West African region. Nigeria's role in the ongoing political crisis in Mali and other West African states is associated with the ECOWAS Mechanism for Conflict Prevention and Management[160]. President Muhammadu Buhari's foreign policy strategy makes regional integration a priority within ECOWAS, including free trade, to ensure that a common tariff and currency are achieved by 2020 under Nigeria's guidance and leadership and to maintain strong, close, and frank relationships within the ECOWAS member states[161].

**Nigeria and Conflict Management in ECOWAS.** During the formation of the Economic Community of West African States Ceasefire Monitoring Group (ECOMOG), President Ibrahim Babangida was seen to have spearheaded the formation of the group, essentially because of Nigeria's political will to determine and influence its subregion. According to Daniel (2007), Nigeria's leadership status in West Africa and Africa at large is a result of its endowment of human and natural resources, which encouraged Nigeria's manifest destiny to remain more about influence than power.

Moreover, the ECOMOG was initiated as a result of the Liberian conflict, which became a school of thought for ECOWAS and its member states. Despite that, the international community stood aloof while Liberians were left to their fate at the commencement of the conflict. In line with this judgment, President Ibrahim Babangida, who posed as the most influential leader in the subregion, spearheaded the move for the formation of ECOMOG to intervene in the Liberian conflict[162]. According to Ochoche (1999), the decision to establish the regional intervention force, ECOMOG, was reached at the first session of the standing committee on Liberia held in Banjul, Gambia, in August 1990 by the leaders of ECOWAS, who were in their presence.

To amplify this, Gani (1993) identifies the role Nigeria played in the formation of ECOMOG, which he believed was a good sign for

---

[160] *ECOWAS Protocol Relating to the Mechanism for Conflict Prevention, Mechanism, Management, Resolution, Peacekeeping and Security, 1999.*
[161] *Manifesto of All Progressive Congress. All Rights Reserved. 2014.*
[162]*Ibid*

West–Africa security architecture. However, he believed that the Economic Community of West African States Monitoring Group (ECOMOG), which posed an indigenous regional mechanism for conflict management, had succeeded in quelling several civil wars in West Africa because of Nigeria's involvement. According to Obi (2009), the Economic Community of West African States Monitoring Group (ECOMOG) troops, which were sent to Liberia as a regional peace interventionist force, were largely made up of Nigerian troops and mainly funded by the Nigerian Government.

It could be argued that the Nigerian leading role in ECOMOG was justified by the belief that no sacrifice was too great in the cause of peace and greater political and economic integration of the West African subregion[163]. The critics, however, believed it was a waste of resources by the Babangida administration and that the Nigerian soldiers deployed to the ECOMOG ceasefire mission in Liberia were sent to assist Babangida's friend, Samuel Doe, to remain in power (Fafowora, 2018) but the Babangida administration denied the allegation and claimed that its administration was never subjective to the political conflict in Liberia[164].

Subsequently, during General Sani Abacha's reign in 1993, ECOWAS remained his area of focus, and ECOMOG was the most important regional cooperative unit, intervening in every conflicting area in the West African region. While the disorderliness of the Liberian civil war led Ghana and other major participants in the peacekeeping mission to threaten to pull out, General Sani Abacha remained resolute. In Adeniji (1997), the ECOMOG successes were attainable because of Nigeria's involvement and leadership role in the regional intervention force, which was seen as a good counterbalance to its pariah status in the international community at that time.

For emphasis, during the summit in Yamoussoukro, Ivory Coast in March 1998, the ECOWAS Foreign Ministers reached a consensus on the recommendation for ECOMOG to officially take up peacekeeping operations in West Africa. According to Abegunrin (2003), the Yamoussoukro accord recognised the dominant role that Nigeria

---

[163] *Daily Champion, Lagos, Nigeria, December 24, 1990.*
[164] *Sunday Times, Lagos, Nigeria, October 7, 1990.*

played in the subregional intervention force, which has produced a positive result. Perhaps what the Nigerian troops contributed to ECOMOG tells the story of Nigeria's enormous contribution in relation to member states.

**Table 1: List of ECOMOG commander(s) in Liberia**

| Commander | Country | Title | Date(s) |
|---|---|---|---|
| Lt-Gen. Arnold Quainoo | Ghana | Force Commander | July 1990 – Sept. 1990 |
| Maj-Gen. Joshua Dogonyaro | Nigeria | Field Commander | Sept. 1990 - February 1991 |
| Maj-Gen. Rufus Kupolati | Nigeria | Field Commander | February 1991 – Sept. 1991 |
| Maj-Gen. Ishaya Baku | Nigeria | Field Commander | Sept. 1991- October 1992 |
| Maj-Gen. Tunji Olurin | Nigeria | Field Commander | October 1992 - October 1993 |
| Maj-Gen. John Shagaya | Nigeria | Field Commander | Oct. 1993 - December 1993 |
| Maj-Gen. John Mark Inienger | Nigeria | Field Commander | December 1993 - August 1996 |
| Maj-Gen. Victor Malu | Nigeria | Force Commander | August 1996 - January 1998 |
| Maj-Gen. Timothy Shelpidi | Nigeria | Force Commander | January 1998 - March 1999 |
| Maj-Gen. Felix Mujakperuo | Nigeria | Force Commander | 1999 |

**Table 2: List of ECOMOG troops in Liberia Technical Team**

| Country | Number of a dispatched soldier(s) | Date(s) |
|---|---|---|
| Nigeria | 4908 | January 13, 1995 |
| Ghana | 1028 | January 13, 1995 |
| Guinea | 609 | January 13, 1995 |
| Tanzania | 747 | January 13, 1995 |
| Uganda | 760 | January 13, 1995 |
| Sierra Leone | 359 | January 13, 1995 |
| The Gambia | 10 | January 13, 1995 |
| Mali | 10 | January 13, 1995 |
| Total dispatched | 8,431 | January 13, 1995 |

**Table 2. Number of EOCOMOG dispatched soldier(s) to Liberia**

## Table 3: List of ECOMOG humanitarian assistance to Liberian refugees

| Country | Number of refugees (s) | Date(s) |
|---|---|---|
| Cote d'Ivoire | 367,300 | October 31, 1995 |
| Guinea | 395,000 | October 31, 1995 |
| Ghana | 14,000 | October 31, 1995 |
| Sierra Leone | 4,600 | October 31, 1995 |
| Nigeria | 4000 | October 31, 1995 |
| Total number of Liberian refugees | 784,900 | October 31, 1995 |

**Table 3. A number of Liberian refugees spread across the Western African region**

The above chronological lists of ECOMOG show the deployment of military commanders, the number of dispatched soldiers, and the countries where most of the Liberia refugees seek asylum[165]. However, Tables 1, 2, and 3 show that Nigeria played an active role in ECOMOG peacekeeping operations in Liberia. Nigerian military commander Joshua Dogonyaro took charge of the affairs of the ECOMOG belly two months after the deployment of the ECOMOG troops to Liberia, which in turn produced the expected result as required by the ECOWAS.

Interestingly, the ECOMOG developments began with the intervention in the Liberian civil war in 1990, which claimed the lives of almost 150,000 civilians and led to a complete breakdown of law and order. It displaced scores of people, both internally and outside the borders, resulting in some 784,900 refugees in neighbouring countries, such as Cote d'Ivoire, Ghana, Guinea, Sierra Leone, and Nigeria[166]. To buttress this, Yurtaev (2021) argues that the civil wars in Africa have produced many displaced people as refugees. He claims that if these persons belong to the side of the enemy, their right to asylum is usually denied. According to Ajayi (2004), in 1995, 1996, and 1997, Nigeria contributed whopping sums of 75 percent, 85 percent,

---

[165] *ECOMOG in Liberia. UNOMIL Resolution 972, 1995.*
[166] *The End of the Cold War the Economic Community of West African States. ECOMOG Intervened in Sierra Leone and Liberia.*

and 82 percent of troops, respectively, to the ECOMOG peacekeeping force.

Furthermore, Nigeria's diplomatic and military contributions towards the ECOMOG intervention have shaped the force processes and outcomes throughout Liberia[167] and the Sierra Leone[168] peacekeeping missions. For clarity, the change in ECOMOG field commander from Ghanaian to Nigerian within months of the deployment of the troops was in accordance with Nigeria's input, and the failure of the Ghanaian-led force to prevent the murder of Samuel Kanyan Doe, in turn, encouraged Nigerians to take over the command in 1999. In Prkic (2000) view, after the death of Samuel Kanyan Doe, successive ECOMOG field commanders were Nigerians who were directly responsible for the Nigerian Ministry of Defence. Adibe (2002) claimed that the ECOWAS members in August 1997 introduced an interposition force, ECOMOG II, to assist in the reinstatement of the legitimate government of President Ahmad Tejan Kabbah of Sierra Leone. Again, Nigeria's participation was outstanding; the bulk of the force was formed by Nigerian troops, and all the commanders were Nigerian[169].

Below is a list of ECOMOG commander(s) in Sierra Leone.

| Commander | Country | Title | Date(s) |
|---|---|---|---|
| Major General Gabriel Kamber | Nigeria | Force commander | 2000 |
| Brigadier General Abu Ahmadu | Nigeria | Force commander | 2000 |
| General Maxwell Khobe | Nigeria | Force commander | 1999 |
| Major General Felix Mujakperuo | Nigeria | Force commander | 1999 |
| Brigadier-General Abdul One Mohammed | Nigeria | Force commander | 1998 |

Table 1. Number of ECOMOG commander(s) in Sierra Leone

---

[167] *Lome Ceasefire Agreement 1991. Agreement on Cessation of Hostilities and Peaceful Settlement of Conflict between the Armed Forces of Liberia, and The National Patriotic Front of Liberia, and the Independent National Patriotic Front of Liberia.*

[168]*Lome Ceasefire Agreement 1999. Peace Agreement Between the Government of Sierra Leone and the Revolutionary United Front of Sierra Leone.*

[169]*The ECOWAS in peace and security in West Africa. Peacekeeping in a bad neighborhood. Accord. AJCR 2009/3.*

According to Adebanjo (2008) out of the 13000 troops deployed to ECOMOG between 1998 and 1999, Nigeria contributed 12000 troops. He dismissed the argument against general assumptions that the reason behind Nigeria's involvement in Sierra Leone is to prove its line reasoning. However, he believed that the reason Nigeria involved its military and foreign missions in Sierra Leone was to exercise its leadership role in the subregion.

Subsequently, on the role of the ECOMOG peacekeeping mission Denisova (2015) claimed that the ECOMOG's role in quelling the military and political crises in Liberia and Sierra Leone became successful because of Nigeria's involvement in the process. While Bokeriya (2018) argued that the ECOMOG's vital role in the peacekeeping mission in Liberia was a result of the mandate given by ECOWAS, which served as an instrument of a dual nature. On the one hand, it considered restoring peace, maintaining security, strengthening governance, and the rule of law, but on the other hand, it had weaknesses, unclear ambiguity, or a lack of peacekeeping potential.

Abegunrin (2003) revealed several sources recorded on Nigeria's expenditure to ECOMOG. He claimed that a source recorded Nigeria's expenditure at a total of US$1 billion beyond the original ECOMOG budget of US$500 million, while another source estimated Nigeria's total expenditure at over US$2.8 billion. Meanwhile, Nigeria is reputed by yet another source to have spent in excess of US$4 billion on a peacekeeping mission in Liberia and Sierra Leone, and likewise expended the sum of US$1 million daily on Sierra Leone alone. Osita (2006) argued that the total cost of expenditure that Nigeria spent on the ECOMOG peacekeeping mission in the Mano River Union is estimated at US$8 billion.

Below is a list of Nigeria's military expenditure as a percentage and in constant US$m., of government spending from 2000 to 2022.

| Year(s) | Percentage (%) Internal | Percentage (%) External | Percentage (%) Total | Constant US$m. |
|---------|------------------------|------------------------|---------------------|----------------|
| 2000 | 0.5% | 1.7% | 2.2% | 942m |
| 2001 | 0.8% | 1.7% | 2.5% | 1342m |
| 2002 | 1.0% | 3.9% | 4.9% | 2026m |
| 2003 | 0.6% | 1.9% | 2.5% | 1247m |
| 2004 | 0.5% | 2.2% | 2.7% | 1215m |
| 2005 | 0.4% | 1.8% | 2.2% | 1073m |
| 2006 | 0.3% | 2.5% | 2.8% | 1118m |
| 2007 | 0.4% | 1.6% | 2.0% | 1299m |
| 2008 | 0.5% | 2.9% | 3.4% | 1824m |
| 2009 | 0.5% | 2.8% | 3.3% | 1896m |
| 2010 | 0.5% | 2.7% | 3.2% | 2226m |
| 2011 | 0.6% | 2.7% | 3.3% | 2478m |
| 2012 | 0.5% | 3.0% | 3.5% | 2183m |
| 2013 | 0.5% | 2.9% | 3.4% | 2099m |
| 2014 | 0.4% | 2.8% | 3.2% | 1908m |
| 2015 | 0.4% | 3.4% | 3.8% | 1861m |
| 2016 | 0.4% | 3.9% | 4.3% | 1798m |
| 2017 | 0.4% | 3.2% | 3.6% | 1719m |
| 2018 | 0.5% | 3.5% | 4.0% | 2028m |
| 2019 | 0.5% | 3.1% | 3.6% | 1860m |
| 2020 | 0.6% | 4.4% | 5.0% | 2403m |
| 2021 | 1.0% | 4.2% | 5.2% | 4466m |
| 2022 | 0.6% | 4.5% | 5.1% | 2771m |

**Table 1. Number of Nigeria's military expenditures as a percentage mission and in constant US$m., of government spending 2000–2022[170].**

The above chronological list best explains various aspects of Nigeria's military expenditure from 2000 to 2022, both at the domestic and international levels. Apparently, it is believed that Nigeria incurred more costs for conflict resolution and peacekeeping on foreign missions than domestic intervention. It is a clear example that Nigeria is committed to its region and Africa in general[171].

The successive governments in Nigeria over the years have contributed greatly to the West African peacekeeping mission, especially through the ECOWAS–ECOMOG comparative

---

[170]Nigeria Military Expenditure Database. SIPRI. 19 May 2008.; The World Bank. Country Data. IBRD-IDA. 19 May 2008.

[171]*Nigeria Military Expenditure Database. SIPRI. 19 May 2008.; The World Bank. Country Data. IBRD-IDA. 19 May 2008.*

intervention force, which has fostered relations among conflicting parties and contributed to the progress and development of the West African region through the extension of the African continent[172]. However, Nigeria's contribution to peacekeeping operations in Liberia and Sierra Leone was never for its own interest but to justify its leadership role in West Africa. Nevertheless, the Nigerian government must strengthen its political, military, and economic capacities to maintain regional hegemony, which would automatically pave the way for the country to assume continental leadership.

**ECOMOG Challenges:** The Anglophone ECOWAS members established ECOMOG in 1990 to intervene in the civil war in Liberia. In spite of the commitment of ECOMOG troops in the Liberian civil war, the war lingered from 1989 to 1996 due to the political disagreement among ECOWAS members and conditions given by Charles Taylor, the leader of the National Patriotic Front Rebel Army. Although the Economic Community of West African States did not expect that most of its peacekeeping mission, or rather, the intervention process in Liberia, would become a long–drawn–out affair, rather, anticipate a short, surgical police action; however, the nature of the conflict itself posits a seemingly simple solution., though the immediate cause of the conflict was the incursion of the Charles Taylor National Patriotic Front Rebel Army from Cote d'Ivoire (Liebenow, 1969).

According to ECOWAS members, President Ibrahim Babangida and his counterparts from Sierra Leone and Guinea, etc., the rebel invasions were an act of thuggery that should have been repelled quite well by the Armed Forces of Liberia (AFL). Thus, the Armed Forces of Liberia's failure to quell these raids suggested a fundamental weakness in the ability of the central government in Monrovia, which

---

[172] *ECOWAS,SMC Decision A/DEC.1/8/90, On the Cease-Fire and Establishment of an ECOWAS Cease-Fire Monitoring Group for Liberia, 21 O.J. ECOWAS Spec. Supp. 6.1992.; Lome Ceasefire Agreement 1991. Agreement on Cessation of Hostilities and Peaceful Settlement of Conflict between the Armed Forces of Liberia, and The National Patriotic Front of Liberia, and the Independent National Patriotic Front of Liberia.; Lome Ceasefire Agreement 1999. Peace Agreement Between the Government of Sierra Leone and the Revolutionary United Front of Sierra Leone.*

---

was spearheaded by President Samuel Doe, who failed to effectively govern his people (Adibe, 1997).

However, the solution would be to shore up President Samuel Doe through the provision of arms and ammunition and, if needed, military advisers. However, Nigeria and other concerned countries did precisely that until it became obvious by the summer of 1990 that the invasions were not uncoordinated acts by some actors, who are the tribesmen. Notwithstanding, the Charles Taylor National Patriotic Front Rebel Army, who felt discontented with President Doe's government, intensified its recruitment throughout Liberia to destabilise and frustrate the government of the day (Gani, 1993). Meanwhile, with the impacts of the rebel forces occupying two–thirds of Liberia territory, the President Doe government became helpless and reduced to slight control of a few perimeters around the presidential mansion, and the civilian survivors of the conflict fled in large numbers to neighbouring countries. This, in turn, attracted regional attention to establishing a political and military presence in Liberia.

However, most of the observers expected that the reports emerging from West Africa in the early 1900s, alleging that the National Patriotic Front Rebel Army was trained and equipped by Libya, would trigger the international community, such as the United States, to intervene in the conflict (Osisioma, 1992). In any case, the international community only began by consulting with its African allies with a view to orchestrating a regional response to the Libyan threat, which has been the talk of the town. It was clear that the Organisation of African Unity (OAU) was looked to for leadership. According to Chike (1992), Africa's premier regional arrangement on noninterference in the internal affairs of member states has limited most of the members to willingly intervening in the conflict.

However, the Organisation of African Unity, under the leadership of President Yoweri Museveni of Uganda as Chairman and former Tanzanian foreign minister Salim Ahmed Salim as Secretary–General, did not apply the sui generis character of the Liberian conflict to the norm of non–intervention (Salim, 1995). However, most people believe that their tactic was to liaise with Nigeria, the dominant West African state, to lead a regional force into Liberia within the framework of ECOWAS. The Ibrahim Babangida administration seized on the opportunity not only to exercise statesmanship but also to divert national and international attention away from mounting political abuses and socioeconomic problems in the region.

Subsequently, the chairman of ECOWAS, President Dawda Kairaba Jawara, convened a meeting of ECOWAS heads of state and government in Banjul, Gambia, in 1990 to deliberate on the establishment of the ECOWAS Mediation Committee (SMS), which will be responsible for crisis and conflict management within the West African region (Foltz et al., 1985). Furthermore, the summit accepted the proposal and constituted the membership of the Standing Mediation Committee (SMS) as follows: The Gambia, Ghana, Mali, Nigeria, and Togo. The Community Standing Mediation Committee (SMC) was the final step towards the use of military force by ECOWAS, which was created in May 1990 to intervene in the Liberia conflict[173].

At its inaugural meeting in July 1990, the committee deliberated on the issue of Liberian conflict settlement and agreed on a peace plan with the following tendencies: establishment of an immediate ceasefire by the warring parties; establishment and deployment of the ECOWAS Ceasefire Monitoring Group (ECOMOG) to monitor the observance of the ceasefire by all sides to the conflict; agreement by the parties to the establishment of an interim administration in Monrovia, pending the election of the substantive government; and agreement by the parties to constitute a substantive government through nation–wide elections to be monitored by ECOMOG[174].

Thus, the problem faced by the ECOMOG troops in Liberia has various forms, such as human rights abuses, mediation challenges, and political disagreement among ECOWAS members. These and other factors contributed to the inability of the ECOMOG troops to contain the conflict within Liberia, which in turn spilled over and spread into Sierra Leone, etc.

---

[173] *ECOWAS, SMC Decision A/DEC. 1/8/90, On the Cease-Fire and Establishment of an ECOWAS Cease-Fire Monitoring Group for Liberia, 21 O.J. ECOWAS Spec. Supp. 6. 1992.*

[174] *The Freetown Final Report of 1990. ECOWAS Standing Mediation Committee Ministerial Meeting. In Clement Adibe E. The Liberian Conflict and the ECOWAS & UN Partnership // Third World Quarterly. 1997.*

In accordance with the official reports of the ministerial conference, there had been a substantial disagreement between members of the SMC, on the one hand, and the parties to the conflict, on the other hand, about vital issues in the proposed plan. The issues at stake were the desirability and timing of a ceasefire, the desirability and composition of an interim government, and the usefulness of deploying a regional peacekeeping force.

In the long run, it became inevitable for ECOWAS not to engage with Liberia's warring parties for a peaceful settlement. Moreover, ECOWAS reacted to its initial failure to negotiate a ceasefire between the warring factions, which resulted in an uncontrolled crisis in Liberia. More importantly, the Liberia problem began with the frustration and disagreement between the ministers of the SMC and the rebel leader Charles Taylor, whom they considered contemptuously the principal cause of their failure in Banjul, Gambia.

In the SMC Ministerial Submission, it became ambiguous in the Ministerial Meeting that the Charles Taylor National Patriotic Front Rebel Army (NPFL) was holding on firmly to its initial position of demanding the departure of President Samuel Doe before they could consider any other related matters. However, the constituted committee gained a clear impression that the NPFL had opted for a military solution. In line with this judgment, the Ministerial Meeting decided to push for another course of action that later saw the peaceful end of the Liberian crisis.

Furthermore, a Sub-Committee on Defence Matters was established during the ministerial meeting to address matters concerning the military component to the military arm of the proposed ECOWAS Monitoring Group (ECOMOG) in Liberia. On July 20, 1990, the Sub Committee at last produced a draft of an ECOWAS military intervention force. In presenting the blueprint to the chairman of the ECOWAS summit, President Ibrahim Babangida and the ministers urged the heads of various governments to join hands in bringing the Liberian conflict to a speedy and peaceful end.

Subsequently, the leaders of the SMC states scheduled a meeting in Banjul, Gambia, on August 7, 1990, to adopt Decision A/DEC.1/8/90, which contains the following characteristics of what would later be known as the ECOWAS Peace Plan for Liberia: the formation and immediate deployment of ECOMOG to Liberia;

immediate cessation of hostilities by all factions; generalised disarmament of the warring parties by ECOMOG; the formation of an Interim Government of National Unity pending the conduct of general elections; an embargo on the importation and acquisition of arms by the warring parties in Liberia; and establishing an atmosphere for the conduct of general and presidential elections in Liberia[175].

The ECOWAS-ECOMOG peacekeeping mission resulted from the inability of the ECOWAS Mediation Committee (SMC) to resolve its internal problems, such as the desirability and timing of a ceasefire, the desirability and composition of an interim government, and the usefulness of deploying a regional peacekeeping force[176]. The disagreement between the ministers of the SMC and the rebel leader Charles Taylor was a result of the party's decision not to involve third parties in the peace process[177].

Additionally, the problem of ECOWAS-ECOMOG in peace intervention can be traced to the politics and intraregional rivalries between the francophone and anglophone groups in ECOWAS. The seven francophone members (except Guinea) signed the 1978 Non-aggression treaty, which codified in article 1 the refrain from the threat or use of force or aggression against the territorial integrity and political independence of the member states. According to Adebajo, (2004), several developments created divisions and weakened the Francophone members of the ECOWAS. He believed that the divisions in ECOWAS were a result of President Ibrahim Babangida, who used ECOWAS to form a regional intervention force to intervene in Liberia in 1989.

Again, the ECOMOG performance was adversely affected by the problems related to command and control, its ad hoc nature, mediation challenges, poor coordination and harmonisation between

[175] ECOWAS, *Decision A/DEC.1/8/90, Lagos: The Economic Community of West African States, 1990. In Clement Adibe E. T. Liberian Conflict and the ECOWAS & UN Partnership // Third World Quarterly. 1997.*
[176] *The Freetown Final Report of 1990. ECOWAS Standing Mediation Committee Ministerial Meeting. In Clement Adibe E. The Liberian Conflict and the ECOWAS & UN Partnership // Third World Quarterly. 1997.*
[177] *ECOWAS,SMC Decision A/DEC. 1/8/90, On the Cease-Fire and Establishment of an ECOWAS Cease-Fire Monitoring Group for Liberia, 21 O.J. ECOWAS Spec. Supp. 6. 1992.*

the contributing countries, poor coordination between ECOMOG field commanders and ECOWAS, weak political will, and lack of agreement about the nature and role of ECOMOG among West Africa's leaders[178]. Other challenges include resource, capacity, and institutional weaknesses within ECOWAS, human rights abuses, and allegations of corruption and high-handedness against some ECOMOG peacekeepers.

Accordingly, ECOMOG's political challenges can be traced to the initial rejection made by Cote d'Ivoire and Burkina Faso to the ECOWAS peace plan for Liberia but rather joined other francophone countries in the region, namely, Togo and Mali, who stood as an opposition. This division had very serious repercussions not only for the performance of ECOMOG in Liberia peacekeeping but also its stance as a neutral force working to restore peace to the beleaguered country. The division among the francophone and anglophone ECOWAS members has contributed to the inadequacy of the ECOMOG peacekeeping mission. However, the financial aspect and human rights abuses also contributed to the inabilities of the troops to function effectively[179].

**Nigeria's Military Diplomacy in Africa:** The Nigerian Army has since been actively involved in the management of regional and continental peace, either under the Organisation of African Unity, currently the African Union, or a specific responsible regional security organisation such as ECOWAS-ECOMOG. To buttress this, Kiseleva (1972) argued that Nigeria has traditionally played and continues to play an important political, economic, and military role in West Africa and, by extension, the African continent. She claimed that Nigeria occupies a leading position in ECOWAS and any other subregional organisation in West Africa. Garuba (1987) argued that Nigeria's increased moral stature and greater economic power have positioned the country to continue to play a leadership role on the continent.

---

[178] *Report of the ECOWAS Workshop. Lessons from ECOWAS. Peacekeeping Operations:1990 – 2004. Accra, 10 – 11 February 2005.*

[179] *Convention on the Rights of the Child. General Assembly resolution 44/25 of 20 November 1989.*

Similarly, successive governments in Nigeria over the years have continuously designed, shaped, and maintained a foreign policy that has continued to have impacts on the African continent. This could be seen in the assertion made by Prime Minister Tafawa Balewa in his inaugural speech on 7 October 1960, at the Plenary of the 15th Regular Session of the United Nations General Assembly, exactly six days after Nigeria gained independence and became the 99th member of the organisation declared that Nigeria hoped to work with all African countries for the progress of Africa and to assist in bringing all African territories to a state of responsible independence and help in finding a lasting solution to the problem affecting Nigeria's immediate neighbours.

This statement demonstrated Nigeria's commitment to bringing about cooperation, progress, and the promotion of regional peace and security. In the early period of Nigeria's independence, this statement is a vindication of Nigeria's expressed determination to adhere to and abide by the purposes and principles of the Organisation of African Unity[180], which superseded the Monrovia group. For clarity, the Nigerian Army participated in a peacekeeping operation during the Congo crisis between 1960 and 1964. General Aguiyi Ironsi led over 6,000 Nigerian troops out of the country for the first time in support of the United Nations Operation in the Congo crisis (Adeniran, 2008). Similarly, when the Tanzania Army revolted against their government in 1964, the Tanzanian government invited the Nigerian Army to assist in suppressing the mutiny.

Again, the Nigerian Army was deployed to Chad in 1978 for a peacekeeping mission. In relation to Nigeria's commitment and sacrifices made to the decolonisation processes in Africa, especially on how the Nigerian Airforce was actively involved in the evacuation of refugees back to Zimbabwe from various frontline states where they had gone into exile during the run–up to the First Zimbabwean election to enable them to participate in it (Peter et al., 1989).

---

[180] *The AU Protocol, Constitutive Act, Supra note in, art 5 (2). The African Union Peace and Security Council (AU PSC) was Established under the Protocol Relating to the Establishment of the Peace and Security Council of the African Union, 9 July 2002.*

Other areas where Nigeria's has participated in the maintenance of peace and security in Africa were the eradication of colonialism and white minority rule in countries such as Angola, Guinea–Bissau, Mozambique, Namibia, and South Africa, its aid to countries like Angola, Benin, Botswana, Zambia, and Zimbabwe; and its peacekeeping in countries such as Liberia, Sierra Leone, and the Democratic Republic of Congo (Sanda, 2012).

During the Olusegun Obasanjo regime as a Military Head of State spanning between 1976 and 1979, Nigeria was actively involved in West Africa conflict resolution (Aworawo, 2016). Although the Olusegun Obasanjo regimes were intimidating and radical, they were committed to Nigeria and its subregion. The regime places more emphasis on regional and continental development than the previous government. For the first time in Nigeria's history, Nigeria looked at the United States and Britain straight in the eyes and not only recognised the Nationalist Popular Movement for the Liberation of Angola (MPLA) in Angola but also donated a huge amount of money to the government-led party against the will of the Western World (Garuba, 1987).

In this light, Vladimir et al. (2013) argued that the Union of Soviet Socialist Republics (USSR) engaged in a strategic alliance with the Popular Movement for the Liberation of Angola, which was contrary to the decisions of some great power states, such as the United States and Great Britain. He believed that the strategic alliance between both countries helped to survive South Africa's military incursions in Angola territory in support of its major adversary, the National Union for the Total Independence of Angola, in the 1970s and 1980s. Nwalie (2021) claimed that the USSR participated in the Nigeria-Biafra war. He argued that bilateral relations between Russia and African states have existed since the1960s. Filippov (2020) argued that the African quest for continent peace has encouraged Mali to invite the Russian Wagner Group.

However, the activities of the Boko Haram insurgence in the northern part of Nigeria, led by President Goodluck Jonathan in 2013, contributed 900 troops of the total force of 3300 military troops estimated by ECOWAS to savage the Mali conflict[181]. Again, Nigeria's role in the subregional and continental intervention forces cannot be wished away. However, Nigeria's interest in conflict settlement and peace and sustainability in Africa in general can also be linked to its national interests. For instance, since Nigeria gained independence in 1960 from Great Britain, Nigeria has been playing a vital role in conflict resolution in Africa.

To amplify this, Adebajo (2002a), who has frequently equated Nigeria's peace process in West Africa and Africa to Pax Nigeriana, which is believed to have been created by Bolaji Akinyemi, Nigeria's former foreign affairs minister, to depict Nigeria's efforts at drafting the charter of the OAU. However, Pax Nigeriana is arguably explained to represent Nigeria's ambition at playing a political, economic, and military role in Africa and not an adventure for a Greater Nigeria, as many have argued (Adebajo, 2010).

Meanwhile, Nigeria's contributions and role towards Africa conflict resolution are conceived out of its military capacity, natural endowment, and geopolitics, which have induced the state of Nigeria to successfully influence the West African region[182]. Finally, Nigeria's involvement in the maintenance of peace and security in Africa has been crucial to the existence of the continent but has also produced significant tensions between Nigeria's and other African states, especially the Francophone states, apparently because of Nigeria's military capacity, geopolitical and huge financial donations to regional organisations, such as ECOWAS and the African Union.

---

[181] *Nigeria's Role in the Mali Intervention. Council on Foreign Affairs Relations. 2013.*
[182] *ECOWAS Protocol Relating to the Mechanism for Conflict Prevention, Mechanism, Management, Resolution, Peacekeeping.; Buhari Report in ECOWAS Final Summit. Final Communique: Forty-Eighth Ordinary Session of the ECOWAS Authority of Heads of State and Government. 2015.*

# Chapter Three

## Nigeria's Relations with Major Powers

### 3.1 Nigeria-UK Relations

Since independence in 1960, Nigeria has maintained strong relations with the United Kingdom (UK), its former colonial master. The United Kingdom (UK) is now one of Nigeria's strongest allies, and as such, its security issues are of great concern to London. Nigeria's location on the edge of the Sahel, a region that has seen an alarming rise in terrorist activities, leaves it vulnerable to cross-border activity by insurgents. Its struggles with home-grown insurgents are considered a potential threat to global security. The UK, like many of Nigeria's allies, is worried that the increased presence of terrorist groups in the Islamic State's country could become a threat way beyond Nigeria's borders[183].

However, since the establishment of Nigerian diplomatic relations with the United Kingdom on October 1, 1960, Nigeria-UK bilateral relations have been filled with multidimensional content in the political, diplomatic, defense, economic, and social spheres. The political and diplomatic dialogue between the two states is facilitated by their active cooperation through their membership in international organisations. In particular, relations between the two states are steadily developing through their membership in the Commonwealth of Nations. Based on the common values that the people of Nigeria share with the countries of the Commonwealth, great importance is attached to this organisation in line with Nigeria's foreign policy. For example, President Olusegun Obasanjo (1976-1979; 1999-2007) explained that during the Nigerian civil war in 1967, the Commonwealth of Nations was the first international organisation that intervened in the crisis, and "thereafter, the Commonwealth took a stand to support the maintenance of Nigeria's territorial integrity. The Commonwealth's decision influenced the attitude of other

---

[183] *An Assessment Of Britain's Relations With Nigeria In 2018.*

international organisations and leading world powers, which contributed immensely to Nigeria's survival"[184].This explains why Nigeria`s foreign policy attaches great importance to the Commonwealth of Nations as an organisation.

High-level meetings, including the visits of Prime Minister Theresa May and Prince Charles (now King Charles III) with his wife to Nigeria on August 29, 2018 and November 6, 2018, respectively, show the deepening diplomatic ties between Nigeria and the United Kingdom[185]. In addition, Prime Minister T. May's visit to Nigeria led to the creation of two documents, namely the Nigeria-United Kingdom Security and Defense Partnership and the Nigeria-United Kingdom Economic Development Forum[186].

The Nigerian-UK interaction is also supported by defence cooperation. This aspect is viewed by the two sides as a basis for partnership in view of the continuing problem of the insurgency in Nigeria and the activities of terrorist groups as well as drug cartels. In 2006, the UK established Operation West Bridge, a law enforcement programme that tackles drug trafficking in the West African region[187]. The operation was initiated in Ghana and later in Nigeria and has since resulted in the combined seizures of many kilogrammes of cocaine, heroin and cannabis. The UK provided around £22m to help Nigeria address the humanitarian exigencies caused by Boko Haram[188]. In addition, the UK has also assisted Nigeria in training more than 10,000 Nigerian military personnel in the following areas: military skills, civil military affairs, media operations, command and leadership, as well as improvised explosive devices (IEDs) awareness. The UK has also provided support to Nigerian military training schools and establishments, as well as supporting Nigerian military intelligence. The

---

[184] *Lecture Delivered by HE Chief Olusegun Obasanjo, President of Nigeria "The Commonwealth in the 21st Century: Prospects and Challenges" Institute of Education, University of London, Tuesday 15 March 2005.*

[185] *Official document of the Nigeria High Commission, London, United Kingdom on Nigeria-United Kingdom Bilateral Relations, 16 October 2018.*

[186] *Ibid.*

[187] *United Nations Office on Drugs and Crime: "Drug Trafficking As A Security Threat In West Africa" November 2008.*

[188] *Official document of the Nigeria High Commission, London, United Kingdom on Nigeria-United Kingdom Bilateral Relations, 16 October 2018.*

visit to Nigeria by Prime Minister Theresa May in August 2018 reaffirms their long-standing relations and is a testimony of their commitment to fighting terrorism. "We are determined to work side by side with Nigeria to help them fight terrorism, reduce conflict, and lay the foundations for future stability and prosperity that will benefit us all"[189].

**Economic Relations:** relations between Nigeria and the United Kingdom are also improving in the economic area. As one of the largest economies in Africa and the 10th largest exporter of crude oil, which is the most basic commodity in the world, Nigeria, as a member of the Commonwealth of Nations, has the advantage of selling its products to both members and non-members[190]. Several factors contribute to the relationship between Nigeria and the UK but trade is considered the leading factor. Data from Birmingham City University shows that "UK exports account for a larger share of imports from Nigeria (4.4% in 2016) compared to imports from the EU - 3.8% in 2016" (Hearne, 2017). The economic interest is also reflected in the interaction between Nigeria and the United Kingdom through the Commonwealth of Nations. The Commonwealth Office in Nigeria works with the Nigerian government to strengthen the capacity of the economy, youth development, human rights-related issues, and electoral support. Nigeria continued to be an active member of the Commonwealth, and the primary objective of its membership is to cultivate the organisation in a manner that would promote its socio-economic agenda. Nigeria is a member of the Commonwealth Ministerial Taskforce of Twelve Foreign Ministers on the Reform of the Commonwealth, and the country has continued to participate in various meetings convened to consider the draft charter of the organisation in line with the recommendations of the Eminent Persons Group (EPG)[191].

Furthermore, the total trade in goods and services (exports plus imports) between the UK and Nigeria was £7.6 billion at the end of

---

[189] BBC, London, *Theresa May offers Nigeria help with security and anti-trafficking. 29 August 2018.*
[190] *Department for International Trade (2016).Exporting to Nigeria. London.*
[191] *Ministry of Foreign Affairs of Nigeria, Nigeria-Commonwealth of Nations relations.*

Q1 2022, an increase of 48.4%, or £2.5 billion, in current prices from the end of Q1 2021.

Total trade in goods and services (exports plus imports) between the UK and Nigeria was £7.6 billion at the end of Q1 2022, an increase of 48.4%, or £2.5 billion, in current prices from the end of Q1 2021. Of this £7.6 billion: Total UK exports to Nigeria amounted to £4.3 billion as at the end of Q1 2022 (an increase of 31.6% or £1.0 billion in current prices, compared to the end of Q1 2021); total UK imports from Nigeria amounted to £3.3 billion as at the end of Q1 2022 (an increase of 78.1% or £1.4 billion in the end of Q1 2021). Nigeria was the UK's 37th largest trading partner in Q1 2022, accounting for 0.4% of total UK trade[192]. In 2021, the outward stock of foreign direct investment (FDI) from the UK in Nigeria was £3.4 billion, accounting for 0.2% of the total UK outward FDI stock. In 2021, the inward stock of foreign direct investment (FDI) in the UK from Nigeria was £806 million[193].

---

[192]*Trade data sourced from the latest ONS publication of UK total trade: all countries seasonally adjusted data.*
[193]*Investment data sourced from the ONS ad-hoc data release if not provided in the latest ONS main FDI release.*

## Summary of trade and investment statistics for Nigeria

### Below is a chronological list of UK market share in Nigeria

| Trade | Value in 2022 | Change from 2021 |
|---|---|---|
| Total trade: | £7.6billion | an increase of 48.4% or £2.5 billion |
| Ranking out of all the UK's trading partners | 37th | |
| Total UK exports: | £4.3 billion | an increase of 31.6% or £1.0 billion |
| Ranking out of all the UK's export partners | 30th | |
| UK exports in goods (percentage of total UK exports that were goods) | £1.4 billion (32.9%) | a decrease of 19.7% or £346 million |
| UK exports in services (percentage of total UK exports that were services) | £2.9 billion (67.1%) | an increase of 91.7% or £1.4 billion |
| Total UK imports: | £3.3 billion | an increase of 78.1% or £1.4 billion |
| Ranking out of all the UK's import partners | 43rd | |
| UK imports in goods (percentage of total UK imports that were goods) | £2.2 billion (66.6%) | an increase of 76.3% or £949 million |
| UK imports in services (percentage of total UK imports that were services) | £1.1 billion (33.4%) | an increase of 81.8% or £494 million |
| Total UK market share | 7.0% | an increase of 1.2 percentage points |
| UK market share for goods only | 3.4% | a decrease of 0.7 percentage points |
| UK market share for services only | 18.1% | an increase of 6.9 percentage points |

**UK Foreign Direct Investment (FDI) with Nigeria**

| UK FDI | Value in 2021 | Change from 2020 |
|---|---|---|
| Total UK outward FDI | £3.4 billion | a decrease of 19.2% or £815 million |
| Total UK inward FDI | £806 million | an increase of 2.4% or £19 million |

| Economic statistics and projections using gross domestic product (GDP) for Nigeria | | | |
|---|---|---|---|
| Economic statistics | 2020 | 2021 | 2022 |
| Economic growth, using GDP in real terms, compared to the previous year | -1.8% | 3.6% | 3.3% |
| GDP per capita in $USD (in thousands) | 2.1 | 2.1 | 2.2 |

Table 1. Trade and investment statistics between Nigeria and the UK from 2020 and 2022 Q1 years[194]

The above data showcase trade and investment statistics between Nigeria and the UK from 2020 to 2022 as of the end of the Q1 year. However, it is believed that some of the recent increases in UK trade values will be partly due to price increases.Total trade in goods and services (exports plus imports) between the UK and Nigeria was £7.6 billion as of the end of Q1 2022, an increase of 48.4%, or £2.5 billion, in current prices from the end of Q1 2021. At the end of Q1 2022, total UK exports to Nigeria amounted to £4.3 billion (an increase of 31.6%, or £1.0 billion in current prices, compared to the end of Q1 2021). Of all UK exports to Nigeria at the end of Q1 2022, £1.4 billion (32.9%) were goods and £2.9 billion (67.1%) were services. As of the end of Q1 2022, UK exports of goods to Nigeria decreased by 19.7%, or £346 million, in current prices compared to the end of Q1 2021, while UK exports of services to Nigeria increased by 91.7%, or £1.4 billion, in current prices compared to the end of Q1 2021. As of the end of Q1 2022, total UK imports from Nigeria were £3.3 billion (an increase of 78.1% or £1.4 billion in current prices compared to the end of Q1 2021). Of all UK imports from Nigeria at the end of Q1 2022, £2.2 billion (66.6%) were goods and £1.1 billion (33.4%) were services. In the same period, UK imports of goods from Nigeria increased by 76.3%, or £949 million, in current prices, compared to the end of Q1 2022, while UK imports of services from Nigeria increased by 81.8%, or £494 million, in current prices, compared to the end of Q1 2021.

This means the UK reported a total trade surplus of £994 million with Nigeria, compared to a trade surplus of £1.4 billion as of the end of Q1 2021. At the end of Q1 2022, the UK had a trade in goods

---

[194]*Investment data sourced from the ONS ad-hoc data release if not provided in the latest ONS main FDI release.*

deficit of £781 million with Nigeria, compared to a trade in goods surplus of £514 million at the end of Q1 2021. Meanwhile, at the end of Q1 2022, the UK reported a trade in services surplus of £1.8 billion with Nigeria, compared to a trade in services surplus of £895 million at the end of Q1 2021.

The Nigeria-UK cooperation also covers social issues, with immigration attracting the most attention from the governments. Nigeria had reached out to the Home Office/FCO to provide a clear template or criteria for the repatriation of irregular Nigerian migrants from the UK. However, the implementation of the template has generated some disagreements between the two countries, as the UK consistently demanded that any Nigerian illegally residing in the country must be deported, but Nigeria said such was against the global best practices for a Nigerian born in the UK who has never visited Nigeria but has one or both parents who are Nigerians residing in the country to be deported to Nigeria. However, the UK has offered the Voluntary Return Programme for the return to Nigeria of illegal Nigerian migrants to avoid arrest, detention, and eventual deportation by law enforcement[195]. Notwithstanding this, Nigeria and the UK signed the Memorandum of Understanding (MoU) on Cooperation to Prevent, Supplies, and Punish Trafficking in Persons on 17 November, 2004[196].

There have been cordial bilateral relations between Nigeria and Britain since the advent of the present political dispensation, as the two countries have aimed at developing and maintaining the importance and longstanding relationship between them with a wide range of political, commercial, security, and economic interest. In addition, both Nigeria and the United Kingdom understand the importance of partnership in their bilateral relations based on mutual understanding and trust, mostly because of their similar legal systems, the same language, and shared histories, among others.

---

[195] *Official document of the Nigeria High Commission, London, United Kingdom on Nigeria-United Kingdom Bilateral Relations, 16 October 2018.*

[196] *Centre for Laws of Nigeria, Treaties of the Federation, www.lawnigeria.com/Treaties.php (accessed on: 6.5.2021).*

**Military Relations**: The National Security Advisors of the United Kingdom and Nigeria hosted the inaugural dialogue in support of our Security and Defence Partnership between 31 January and 2 February 2022, in London. The United Kingdom and Nigeria enjoy a deep and long-standing security and defence relationship, underpinned by our shared history, mutual trust, and shared Commonwealth principles of democratic governance and respect for international humanitarian and human rights law, as well as a shared desire to support regional and international peace and security. Through the dialogue, the United Kingdom and Nigeria agreed to enhance our existing cooperation in the following areas: civilian policing; approaches to stabilisation including civilian-led security and civil-military cooperation, human rights; women and youth; peace and security; defence cooperation and maritime security; serious and organised crimes; drug trafficking; human trafficking; border security; and countering terrorism and violent extremism[197].

Again, the United Kingdom reaffirms its support for long-term defence modernisation and transformation in Nigeria and, in support, offers a refreshed package of leadership training for Nigerian military training institutions and the continuation of a training offer that builds understanding of international human rights and international humanitarian law. The United Kingdom and Nigeria agree to explore future cooperation between the UK Armed Forces and Nigeria's Defence Special Operations Force to build Nigeria's capacity to respond to the range of security challenges it faces effectively and in a human rights-compliant way. The United Kingdom and Nigeria reaffirm our commitment to countering terrorism in Nigeria, including providing agreed-upon necessary training and capacity-building support to Nigeria in her efforts to address terrorists and other insurgent forces in the Northeast region of Nigeria. The United Kingdom and Nigeria affirm our commitment to cooperate on maritime security in the Gulf of Guinea. Nigeria reiterates its commitment to deter, disrupt, and prosecute maritime crime (including piracy and armed robbery against ships) through maritime security operations at sea and to actively participate in the G7 Friends of the

---

[197]*UK-Nigeria Security and Defence Partnership Inaugural Dialogue Communique // gov.ru.*

Gulf of Guinea to this end. The United Kingdom offers support to build Nigeria's maritime capabilities, to continue supporting both the Gulf of Guinea Maritime Collaboration Forum/SHADE mechanism and the Yaoundé Code of Conduct framework, and to collaborate with Nigerians on enhancing port security.

## 3.2 Nigeria-USA Relations

The United States (US) established diplomatic relations with Nigeria in 1960, following Nigeria's independence from the United Kingdom. From 1966 to 1999, Nigeria experienced a series of military coups, excluding the short-lived second republic between 1979 and 1983. The 30-month-long civil war, which ended in January 1970, resulted in 1-3 million casualties. Following the 1999 inauguration of a civilian president, the U.S.-Nigerian relationship began to improve, as did cooperation on foreign policy goals such as regional peacekeeping.

**Economic Relations**: In order to remain in the foreseeable future, the United States (US), the world economic, technological, and scientific leader, decided to cooperate with Nigeria, which positions itself as a giant in Africa. It is important to note that the United States established its diplomatic relations with Nigeria in 1960, after Nigeria gained independence from the United Kingdom. From 1966 to 1999, a series of military coups occurred in Nigeria, excluding the short-lived second republic between 1979 and 1983.[198] Nigeria is currently the largest African economy and the most populous country on the African continent, with an estimated GDP of 398 billion US dollars in 2018, 447 billion US dollars in 2019, 432.2 billion US dollars in 2020, 440.8 billion US dollars in 2021, and 1.085 trillion dollars at the end of 2022, respectively. Despite the fact that the Nigerian economy has become more diversified, crude oil sales continue to be the main source of export revenue. Despite persistent structural weaknesses such as inadequate transport infrastructure, the Nigerian economy continued to grow rapidly for a decade. Growth slowed in 2014, largely

---

[198] *U.S. Department of State. U.S. Relations With Nigeria. URL: https://www.state.gov/u-s-relations-with-nigeria/ (accessed on: 6.5.2021).*

due to falling oil prices, and in 2016 and 2017, Nigeria experienced its first recession for more than two decades before recovering in 2018.[199]

With Nigeria's return to democracy in 1999, bilateral relations between the United States and Nigeria continued to improve, and cooperation on a number of important foreign policy issues, such as maintaining peace in the West African region, was outstanding. It is estimated that one million Nigerians and Nigerian Americans live, study, and work in the United States, and more than 25,000 Americans live and work in Nigeria.[200]

With the joint participation of Secretary of State Hillary Clinton and the Nigerian secretary under the government of the federation, Yayal Ahmed, a bilateral commission of the United States and Nigeria was opened—an official obligation to conduct bilateral negotiations on four key areas: energy and investment; agriculture and food security; good governance, transparency, and integrity; the Niger Delta; and regional security. President Yar'Adua visited President George W. Bush at the White House on December 13, 2007. During her first official trip to Africa, Secretary of State Clinton visited Nigeria on August 12, 2009. President Jonathan met with President Barack Obama at the White House on June 8, 2011.

Nigeria is currently the largest US trading partner in sub-Saharan Africa, mainly due to the high export rate of Nigerian oil, which accounts for 8% of US oil imports, which is half the daily oil production in Nigeria. Nigeria is in fifth place in terms of US oil exports. Bilateral trade in 2010 was estimated at more than 34 billion dollars, which is 51% more than in 2009, mainly due to the restoration of world prices for crude oil. Exports from the United States to Nigeria in 2010 exceeded 4 billion US dollars due to crops (wheat and rice), the automotive industry, oil products, and various equipment. In 2010, US imports from Nigeria totaled more than $30 billion, mostly due to oil.[201] In 2022, the two-way trade in goods between the United States and Nigeria totaled over $8.1 billion.

---

[199] *Nigeria - Central Intelligence Agency. URL:https://www.cia.gov/library/publications/the-world-factbook/geos/ni.html(accessed on: 6.5.2021).*

[200] *U.S. Department of State. U.S. Relations With Nigeria.*

[201] *US oil imports in 2017.*

---

Such products as aluminium, bauxite and cocoa, rubber, waxes, tobacco, and cereals totaled about US$73 million of US imports from Nigeria in 2010. The US trade deficit with Nigeria in 2010 amounted to 26 billion US dollars. In 2010, Nigeria became the 13th largest trading partner of the United States. In turn, the United States is Nigeria's second largest partner after the United Kingdom. And despite the fact that the balance of trade is more favourable for Nigeria, mainly due to oil exports, it is believed that a significant part of US exports to Nigeria come to the country outside of the official statistics of the Government of Nigeria, due to the fact that importers seek to avoid tariffs and Nigerian legislation.

The United States is Nigeria's largest foreign investor. In 2010, US Foreign Direct Investment in Nigeria totaled US$ 5.2 billion. United States FDI to Nigeria is more concentrated in the oil, mining, and wholesale sectors. ExxonMobil and Chevron are the two largest US corporate offshore oil and gas players in Nigeria.

The United States and Nigeria met in the framework of the existing Trade and Investment Framework Agreement (TIFA) in March 2009 to advance the current work programme and raise the issue of improving Nigerian trade policy and market access. Among the issues raised are cooperation in the World Trade Organisation (WTO), export diversification, access to markets, various commercial issues, intellectual property protection, infrastructure and investment issues, as well as trade capacity building and technical assistance[202].

**Decreased US Dependence on Oil Imports in 2018:** In 2018, the United States imported about 9.9 million barrels of petroleum per day, which included 7.8 million barrels of petroleum per day (MMb/d) of crude oil and 2.1 million barrels of petroleum per day of noncrude petroleum liquids and refined petroleum products. Net imports (imports minus exports) of petroleum relative to petroleum consumption are one measure of our reliance on imports to help meet petroleum demand. After generally increasing every year between 1950 and 2005, US total and net petroleum imports peaked in 2005. Even though consumption and imports have increased slightly in recent

---

[202] *Trade and Investment Framework Agreement.*

years, increases in domestic petroleum production and exports have helped to reduce total annual net imports every year since 2005. In 2018, net imports of petroleum averaged 2.3 million barrels of petroleum per day, the equivalent of 11% of total US petroleum consumption and the lowest percentage since 1957[203].

The main obstacles to progress in Nigeria's economic and democratic development are factors such as widespread poverty, internal conflicts, poor governance, poor service delivery, and deep-rooted corruption. Nigeria remains at the bottom of the Human Development Index of the Joint National Development Programme (UNDP). Despite significant success in reforming macroeconomic policies over the past few years, these changes still have not brought tangible improvements in people's lives. Assistance from the United States was aimed at supporting Nigeria in resolving this problem by: improving conditions for regional and international trade; promoting transparent and responsible governance; increasing the professionalism of the military and law enforcement agencies; increasing the growth of the non-oil economy, involving civil society and government partners in the fight against corruption; as well as strengthening health and education systems to provide quality services.

Strong financial and trade potential will be created through financial support for economic growth, and conditions for microfinance and agriculture will be improved. The United States will continue to work actively within the framework of the Global Food Security Response System, which will accelerate proven production, processing, and marketing technologies as well as significantly increase the productivity of selected major food crops. Along with this, the development of the value chain in agriculture will accelerate and job creation through the growth of agribusiness enterprises will be stimulated. Customs and political reforms will improve inter-regional trade, transport links, and unhindered supplies to regional markets, which will ensure compliance with international standards. United States assistance is also focusing on expanding investment opportunities, which is complicated by access to market-based

---

[203] *U.S. domestic petroleum production includes total petroleum field production, renewable fuels and oxygenate plant net production, and refinery processing gain. Preliminary data for 2018.*

financial and commercial services, including microfinance. Assistance from the United States should also help expand access to credit through partnerships with commercial banks and by expanding the capabilities of microfinance institutions. The United States will work with the Central Bank of Nigeria to improve the political environment for micro, small, and medium enterprises.

Current presidential initiatives with Nigeria include the Africa Hunger Eradication Initiative, the Trans-Sahel Counter-Terrorism Programme, the African Growth and Competitiveness Initiative, and fighting the Avian flu. The right of Nigeria to participate in other regional events implies the so-called hunger early warning system; human trafficking; the anti-corruption initiative; as well as the Ambassador's Girls Scholarship Fund. Nigeria is a leading member of PEPFAR, for which around $467 million was allocated in fiscal 2008[204]. However, Nigeria's commitment to these initiatives' would foster and consolidate their positions in maintaining regional and continental leadership. Additionally, Nigeria is an important US security partner in Africa. Nigeria is engaged in intensive efforts to defeat terrorist organisations within its borders, including Boko Haram and ISIS-West Africa (ISIS-WA) (Nwalie et al., 2022). US security cooperation strengthens the capacity of Nigeria's security forces and security institutions to respond effectively to these and other security threats while prioritising the avoidance of civilian harm and promoting respect for human rights. Nigeria is a vital member of the Defeat ISIS (D-ISIS) coalition, and in October 2020, Nigeria co-hosted a virtual D-ISIS conference with the United States.

**Military Relations**: Nigeria is an important US security partner in Africa. Nigeria is engaged in intensive efforts to defeat terrorist organisations within its borders, including Boko Haram and ISIS-West Africa (ISIS-WA). US security cooperation strengthens the capacity of Nigeria's security forces and security institutions to respond effectively to these and other security threats while prioritising the avoidance of civilian harm and promoting respect for human rights. Nigeria is a vital

---

[204] *Nigeria – US Relations. URL:https://www.globalsecurity.org/military/world/nigeria/forrel-us.htm(accessed on: 6.5.2021).*

member of the Defeat ISIS (D-ISIS) coalition, and in October 2020, Nigeria co-hosted a virtual D-ISIS conference with the United States[205].

Military cooperation between Nigeria and the USA is no longer an issue of doubt or debate in academic and defence circles. Since 2001, both the Nigerian and American governments have issued political statements admitting military cooperation but not a military pact. In spite of misgivings about due process, military cooperation has existed between the two countries. Two recent developments are important. The first has to do with the impact of the September 11, 2001, terrorist attacks on the USA. Perhaps the military cooperation with Nigeria became very dear to the USA in 'fighting' terrorism globally. In fact, cooperation is needed with states that harbors terrorists in Islamic communities. If a state is suspect in the eyes of the USA, it invites trouble. The Nigerian leadership, however, has tried quite hard to dissociate itself from harbouring terrorists of any sort.

The other recent event relates to the US suspension of military cooperation with Nigeria. On March 20, 2003, the Federal Ministry for Foreign Affairs Chief Dubem Onyia made a public announcement that linked the withdrawal of military aid to Nigeria's opposition to the US-led war on Iraq. Since then, US-Nigeria military relations have created strains in both the political and defence establishments. Overall, Nigeria means a lot to the USA, and the present strained relations could be temporary, and military cooperation between Nigeria and the USA may be expected to return to normalcy.

### 3.3 Nigeria-China Relations

The People's Republic of China has become an industrialised, scientific, and technological leader among the leading exporters of high-tech products to Nigeria and Africa as a whole. The Chinese market is becoming the main source of economic growth on the African continent, especially in Nigeria. However, China's priorities are to expand the economy to Africa and beyond. Nigeria and the People's

---

[205]*US Relation with Nigeria // US Department of State, 2023. URL: https://www.state.gov/u-s-relations-with-nigeria. (accessed on 26.11.2023)*

Republic of China established official diplomatic relations on February 10, 1971. Relations between the two countries have become closer as a result of international isolation and Western condemnation of the military dictatorships of Nigeria (1970s-1998). Since then, Nigeria has become an important source of oil for China's fast-growing economy, and Nigeria hopes that China will help achieve high economic growth rates to dominate regional and continental leadership, although China has provided extensive economic, military, and political support to Nigeria.

Bilateral relations between the People's Republic of China and Nigeria have reached a new height following the trade agreement signed on 18 July, 2019 between the representatives of the two countries. Nonetheless, both countries have been cooperating in multiple areas since they established diplomatic ties. However, the ties solidified after the agreement between the Nigeria-China Belt and Road Investment Forum held in Hangzhou, Zhejiang, China. Perhaps this would sustain the bilateral trade and investment relations between China and Nigeria for the mutual benefit of both countries[206].

China and Nigeria had similar experiences, and both countries pursued an independent foreign policy of peace. This became the basis of a solid foundation and relations of cooperation between the two countries; however, they both attach importance to each other's concerns and seek common ground while resolving differences as well as continuously enhancing mutual trust. «Good brother, Good friends, and Good partners» Borging, a former Chinese Ambassador to Nigeria, described the historical development of both countries as fruitful despite criticism around the globe (Nwalie, 2020).

**Economic Relations**: China and Nigeria have been good partners in economic and trade relations, always trying to achieve mutual benefits and win-win outcomes. Either during assistance or in the trading process, priority is given to the well-being of people; moreover, encouraging Chinese companies to increase their investment in Nigeria, promote the value added of exported Nigerian products,

---

[206]*Nigeria, China meet to sustain mutual trade relations. URL:https://www.vanguardngr.com/2019/07/ni geria-china-meet-to-sustain-mutual-trade-relations/ (accessed on: 6.5.2021).*

provide more employment opportunities for local people, and therefore enable consistently healthy and sustainable development of bilateral cooperation (Tony, 2008). China remains the most populous country in the world with a population of more than 1.4 billion people, representing 18.59% of the world's population, while Nigeria is the most populous African country with a population of more than 200 million people, according to a 2019 UN report[207]. Both countries are the most densely populated, while African countries are the most densely populated nations. Moreover, it seems that the ties of economic relations between them are being rekindled, especially after the resumption of the summit of the China-Africa Cooperation Forum (FOCAC), which brought enormous and positive changes in both countries and beyond (Nwalie, 2020).

The FOCAC process was conceived in late 1990 as a result of the fact that several African countries proposed to the Chinese authorities the idea of such a forum in order to consolidate and develop Sino-African relations and multilateral cooperation. China's proposal to convene an appropriate group led to the creation of a forum on Sino-African cooperation at a ministerial conference held in Beijing in 2000. Furthermore, more than 80 ministers of China and 44 African countries, as well as representatives of 17 countries attended the summit. Regional and international organisations participated in the first FOCAC Ministerial Conference in Beijing in 2000. The purpose and objective of this event were to create the basis for the development of mutually beneficial, stable, and long-term relations between China and Africa and also provide an institutionalised platform for expanding bilateral exchanges and cooperation (Nwalie, 2020). However, the first FOCAC summit was completed by two documents: one is the Beijing Declaration of the Forum on Sino-African Cooperation, which sets out common positions on a key international issue, and the second is a programme of Sino-African cooperation in economic and social development, which identified a number of measures for cooperation in various fields, from economics and trade to tourism, education, and the environment[208].

---

[207] *UN population prospects 2019.*
[208] *FOCAC:a win-win formula for sino-africa relations?10th October,2000*

**Chinese International Development Assistance in Nigeria:**
Chinese development assistance in Nigeria has focused on economic investment and reconstruction, with specific projects for infrastructure and economic livelihood recovery in post-conflict areas such as the Niger Delta. Chinese investment also focuses on the electric power and energy sector in Nigeria, but investment in this area comes with a great risk of violence and instability, undermining development investment. This risk comes as a result of protests from Niger Delta agitators, who demand fair treatment of allocations from the Nigerian government. The Chinese Ambassador to Nigeria, H.E. Gu Xiaojie, claims that Nigeria is «China's number one engineering market, number two export market, number three trading partner, and major investment destination in Africa»[209]. It is reported that China's foreign direct investment in Nigeria was $85.8 million in 2013 and increased to $116.87 million in 2014.[210] The Nigerian Investment Promotion Commission (NIPC) reports over $3 billion received from China for investment in economic growth areas such as power-sector development, solid minerals, agriculture, rail transportation, and housing infrastructure. [211] For example, a China-Nigeria memorandum of understanding (MOU) was signed for investment in railways, refineries, reindustrialisation, the Mambilla hydro-electric project, and a general increase in trade on September 13, 2016. Likewise, in November 2014, China signed a contract for a $12 billion Nigerian railway project. And most recently, on September 15, 2016, Nigeria and China signed a $23 billion deal for three refineries in Kogi, Lagos, and Bayelsa states.

This relationship resulted in the establishment of the Nigeria-China Business Council following the First Nigeria-China Trade and Investment Forum held in Abuja in September 2016. This forum's participants discussed Chinese investment in Nigeria, which has reached over $80 billion. Nigeria views its relationship with China as one that also benefits its own export needs and its international negotiating prowess. The country is now affectionately known as

---

[209] *Africa Today's Conference on Nigeria-China Relations and Implications for Nigeria's Foreign Policy Concentricism May 8, 2016.*
[210] *Ibid*
[211] *Ibid*

«Africa's China» among international investors. This relationship will enable Nigeria to become a major player in both Africa's and now Asia's markets.

Finally, in 2021, despite the adverse impact of the pandemic, China-Nigeria trade reached 25.68 billion USD, rising 33.3% year on year, and Nigeria's exports to China reached 3.04 billion USD, rising 22.4% year on year. From 2016 to 2021, this bilateral trade increased by nearly 142%. According to uncompleted statistics, in the first ten months of 2022, the bilateral trade volume reached 20.04 billion USD[212]. Currently, Nigeria is China's third-largest trading partner in Africa, and China is Nigeria's largest source of imports.

**Military Relations.** Nigeria and China have shown how to foster military cooperation among nations, that is, to protect, develop, and promote the defence interests of their countries. According to the strategic partnership between the two countries, it is based on the bedrock of shared values, shared interests, and true friendship. They have demonstrated the width and depth of security and defence ties as a model for African relations[213].

However, military-to-military relations are an important component of Nigeria-China cooperation. The Chinese People's Liberation Army (PLA), which has been a strong pillar in safeguarding China's sovereignty, security, and development interests, is an upholder of world peace and human progress and has also been a reliable and sincere partner of Nigeria. Under various frameworks such as the Belt and Road Initiative and Forum for China-Africa Cooperation (FOCAC) and bilateralism since 1971, China has launched programmes that have helped train Nigerian military and security personnel on areas of law and order, UN peacekeeping missions fighting piracy and combating terrorism, and the supply of state-of-the-art equipment such as ICT, drones, patrol vessels, and hardware.

There is also fruitful military exchange under the principle of mutual assistance. Nigerian officers attended military and security

---

[212]*Ministry of Foreign Affairs of the People's Republic of China.*
[213]*Deepening Nigeria-China Military Cooperation // Cable. URL: https://www.thecable.ng/deepening-nigeria-china-military-cooperation. (accessed on 27.11.2023).*

training in China. The joint efforts of the two have strengthened counterterrorism and anti-piracy campaigns in Nigeria. For instance, Nigeria signed a memorandum of understanding with China in 2020 to fight terrorism. There are provisions for free military aid in 2013 and 2016 and the acquisition of defence equipment in 2019, among others. That enabled military aid to the Joint Task Force fighting insurgents in the north-east and bandits in the north-west, and there was also support for security in the Gulf of Guinea.

### 3.4 Nigeria-Russia Relations

Following Nigeria's independence in 1960, the country began diplomatic relations with many countries around the world. Nigeria's relationship with Russia began with the Union of Soviet Socialist Republics (USSR) and has lasted ever since. The first major diplomatic cooperation between both nations was during the Nigerian civil war from 1967 to 1970. The Nigerian government turned to the Soviet Union for military cooperation, which eventually led to its victory in the war. There has been a division among scholars in trying to explain the Soviet help to Nigerian forces. Northedge (1975) argued that the USSR chose to support Nigeria solely to reduce the powers and influence of the Western nations and advance its own. Omotuyi (2018) buttressed this argument by arguing that the Soviet Union saw the Nigerian civil war as a battle between capitalism and socialism. While this argument could hold some truth due to the polarised state of the world in the 1960s, it fails to consider some very important facts. First, Nigeria actually never became a communist country. And there has been no evidence to show that the Soviet Union asked Nigeria to become socialist as a precondition for its support during the war. Other factors could certainly have influenced the Soviet decision. The first of this was that the USSR at the time was one of the world's largest manufacturers of arms, and the Nigerian government was desperately in need of firearms; therefore, cooperation only became a practical economic matter.

Additionally, there was a matter of shared identity between both countries. After Western nations almost unanimously dropped their support for Nigeria, Nigeria immediately fell into the same boat as the USSR: the Western alliance led by the United States of America and

Britain both opposed them. Therefore, rather than a motivation to spread communist beliefs, a shared identity with Nigeria might have motivated the Soviet Union. This behaviour can be explained by the ancient proverb: 'the enemy of my enemy is my friend'. Sarpestein (2004) and Maoz et al. (2007) have documented many instances in international relations where this has motivated countries to work together.

In October 2019, President Buhari and President Putin reached a new agreement to strengthen Nigeria-Russia relations. They reached a mutual opinion that it is crucial to put Nigeria-Russia relations on a fast track and pursue the completion of partially completed and abandoned projects initiated by both countries[214]. The two leaders agreed to start new infrastructure projects and expand trade and investment, security, and military cooperation. In statements made by the two presidents, Nigeria and Russia will work together to improve Nigeria's oil sector's efficiency, which is the backbone of the country's economy[215]. There is an agreement to establish a framework for a joint venture between the Nigerian National Petroleum Corporation (NNPC) and the Russia-based leading oil company, Lukoil, to work towards the prospection of oil deep offshore.

The issue of an uncompleted and abandoned Ajaokuta Steel Rolling Mill was presented by President Buhari. His request for Russia's return to a government-to-government relationship for the completion and commissioning of the plant was accepted by President Vladimir Putin. Moreover, the Russian government agreed to support the development of Nigeria's rail infrastructure by constructing a 1,400-kilometer track from Lagos to the South-South city of Calabar.

The two presidents also addressed partnerships in education and agriculture. The Russian leader Vladimir Putin noted that the Russian government is ready to give additional scholarships to Nigerians.

There has been increased educational cooperation between Russia and Nigeria, and indeed, all of Africa. At the Russia-Africa Summit in 2019, Russia's minister of science and higher wducation, Mikhail

---

[214] *Alfa Shaban, Abdur Rahman "LIST: African presidents, PMs attending Russia - Africa summit". africanews. Retrieved 27 October 2019.*
[215] *Ezere Aturi. President Buhari Meets President Putin in Sochi / WallAfrica News, October 26.*

Kotyukov, reported that there are over 17000 African students studying in Russian universities, 4000 of whom are studying with the help of a scholarship from the Russian government[216].

**Economic Relations:** It is interesting to note that since 2019, after the first Russia-Africa Summit in Sochi, the Nigerian government has hosted several delegates from the Russian business community, taken part in many exhibitions, and is currently experiencing a robust and healthy relationship with the Russian Federation, mostly in the areas of trade and investment. Like most of the other partner nations, Nigeria has seen a rise in trade volume between both nations. During the last 25 years, the exports of Nigeria to Russia have increased at an annual rate of 6.36%, from $8.3M in 1996 to $38.8M in 2021[217]. In 2021, Russia exported products to the tune of over $1 billion to Nigeria. The main products exported from Russia to Nigeria were refined petroleum products worth over 500 million dollars, wheat worth about $500 million, and Fertilizers over $70 million. Finally, key players in the African economy, including Nigeria, have also stepped up their games in the energy sector in partnership with the Russian Federation, with several nuclear plants and energy projects being constructed, even as ROSATOM (Russia's state-owned energy company) has chosen to educate several African students on energy programmes for free.

However, Nigeria is interested in bringing Russian companies into its oil and gas projects, as well as gaining access to their technologies[218]. Russian companies have competencies, and Nigeria has resources, but in order to use them, it needs Russian experience and competencies for extraction. Nigeria's permanent secretary of the Petroleum Resources Ministry and the country's official representative to OPEC, Gabriel Aduda, said at the last Russia-Africa summit in St. Petersburg that both countries must certainly include the transfer of technology and experience in their cooperation in order to work together as partners. According to him, Nigeria has lacked financial resources for many years, but if one considers effective cooperation, it needs project

---

[216] *The Pie News. (2019). African students enrolled in Russian universities on the rise.*

[217] *Second Russia-African summit: Expectations, impact on Nigerian economy // Sept 10, 2023, Vanguard.*

[218]*Nigeria interested in Russian oil and gas technologies // Jul 28, 2023, Interfax. International Information Group*

financing rather than money in the form of loans. He argued that the recent negotiations between both countries would revive Russia's operations in Nigeria.

**Military Relations**: On security and military cooperation, which existed for fifty-nine years of Nigeria's independence, President Buhari agreed to renew the Nigeria-Russia Military Technical Agreement that had lapsed within a short time. This military cooperation agreement is expected to give impetus to further cooperation of military hardware on a government-to-government basis at a lower cost, training of military personnel, modernisation of the armed forces, and renewal of infrastructure and equipment that President Putin promised to undertake. According to President Putin, 2,000 ex-ISIS terrorists joined Boko Haram last year. Furthermore, he expressed his further determination to secure Nigeria and the rest of Africa from this terrorist insurgency.

In recent times, a similar situation has arisen. The Council on Foreign Relations (2021) reported Nigeria's recent deal to buy military equipment from Russia, just after the United States stalled on a $1 billion deal due to alleged human rights violations. The report described the new deal as solely economic or "transactional" and not considered a power play by Moscow. Nevertheless, it can be argued that Russia's history with internal insurgency and the western perceptions of human rights violations in the country are likely bigger motivating factors for this cooperation.

Nigeria has undoubtedly had some military interactions with Russia in the recent past. There was a time when Nigeria attempted to buy US Cobra attack helicopters. However, Washington's attempt was rebuffed in 2014, so Nigeria had to turn to Russia, which had no problem selling Nigeria 21 Mi-35 attack helicopters and 11 Mi-17 utility helicopters. Subsequently, Nigeria made an order for 12 Russian Mi-35M attacks in September 2016 (Sputnik News, 2017). There was a report by the Russian media that there had been plans to sell Nigeria ten Sukhoi Su-30 multirole jet fighters in mid-2017. However, the sales did not seem to have gone through. As earlier noted, Nigeria has been facing the insurgency of Boko Haram since 2009. The group staged several bloody terror attacks, including the 2011 bombing of a UN office in Abuja's capital, which killed 21 people[219]. In April 2014, Boko Haram abducted 276 female students from a government secondary school in the eastern Nigerian town of Chibok.

Along with Nigeria, Niger, Cameroon, and Chad are also currently engaged in military operations to fight Boko Haram. Additionally, the militants have kidnapped thousands of people throughout the years of the insurgency to fund their efforts to introduce Sharia law in the region. In May 2017, Russian Foreign Minister Sergey Lavrov met with his Nigerian counterpart, Geoffrey Onyeama, and ascertained that Russia would further support the Nigerian struggle against the Boko Haram insurgency. Finally, Nigeria-Russia received a boost in 2017 with the signing of the Military Technical Cooperation Agreement (MTCA), which was renewed in August 2021 in Moscow. Nigeria has longstanding and wide-ranging cooperation with Russia in the field of defence. With the signing of the MTCA, it is expected that Nigeria-Russian military technical cooperation will gradually metamorphose from a buyer-seller framework to one that will involve joint research, development, and manufacture of sophisticated defence technologies and systems.

### 3.5 Nigeria-France Relations

France established diplomatic relations with Nigeria on October 1, 1960, following Nigeria's independence. Nigeria has largely enjoyed cordial relations with the European country over the years, with major French companies such as Peugeot, EIF, Total Energies, and Air France having significant historical and contemporary economic presences in Nigeria. The fact that all the countries Nigeria shares land borders with, namely Benin Republic, Niger Republic, and Cameroon, are Francophone further underscores the strategic importance of Nigeria's relationship with France.

Since independence in 1960, economic, political, and diplomatic exchanges have characterised Nigeria-France relations. Relations

---

[219] *Diamond L. Conflict and anxiety in the second Nigeria // Journal of modern African studies. - 2010 Vol. 20(4). P. 629-668.*

between Nigeria and France from 1960 to present have been characterised by a major paradox: a long history of difficult political relations coexists with an even longer history of good economic relations.

In February, April, and December 1960, France exploded three nuclear devices in the Sahara, despite the vehement protests by many of the then newly independent African countries. In retaliation against the unfriendly act, Nigeria gave France 48 hours to close down its Embassy in Lagos and to pack out of the country in early January 1961. The French Embassy in Lagos was to remain closed until October 1965. Nigeria also banned French ships and airplane's from calling at our ports.

This attitude resurfaced in 1962, when Nigeria (following Britain) commenced negotiations with the EEC in order to obtain associate membership with the Community. France systematically opposed Nigeria's admission, presumably on the ground that Nigeria should not enjoy certain privileges until then reserved mainly for Francophone countries[220]. The accord with the EEC was not signed until the 16 July, 1966, two months after the re-establishment of diplomatic relations between Nigeria and France[221].

**Economic Relations:** Nigeria's economic growth and the development of its external commercial trade in the 1970s depended on the 1973/1974 and 1978 increases in the price of petroleum (Nwalie, 2022). One has to remember the important place occupied by petroleum in Nigeria's total exports and in the Nigerian government's revenues. It accounted for not less than 90% of the total revenues from exports and 80% of the total Federal Government of Nigeria's collected revenue. The petroleum boom of the 1970s was important as a catalyst in the economic and commercial relations between Nigeria and France. However, Nigeria found an economic and commercial partner in France, which bought a lot of its crude petroleum. On the

---

[220] IFRA-Nigeria. *French Institute for Research in Africa, Nigeria. URL:* *https://books.openedition.org/ifra/3962?lang=en. (accessed on 27.11.2023)*
[221] Wigwe, *Economic Diplomacy and Nigeria-France Relations // Cable.* *URL:https://www.thecable.ng/wigwe-economic-diplomacy-and-nigeria-france-relations. (accessed on 27.11.2023)*

other hand, France discovered in Nigeria a large market for its finished manufactured products and equipment. France also discovered in Nigeria a reliable source of petroleum that is very far away from the turbulent Middle East and Far East. This development consolidates the economic relations between Nigeria and France.

Moreover, Nigeria receives a series of supports from the French government, such as economic development, security, health, support for the private sector, and agriculture. This has been the practice since the 1960s, when the two states established diplomatic relations. Currently, their focal point between Nigeria and France has been trade and security. Again, French exports to Nigeria consist of refined petroleum products, pharmaceuticals, mechanical, electric, electronic, and computer equipment, and agro-food products, while exports from Nigeria to France are mainly made up of petroleum products. The French Business Report estimated bilateral trade between the two states at €3.6 billion in 2017 (Gbadebo, 2019). The report opined that "Nigeria remains France's leading trading partner in sub-Saharan Africa" and that "Nigeria remains France's fifth-largest supplier of natural hydrocarbons and the leading supplier in sub-Saharan Africa. The stock of French FDI in Nigeria was €6.5 billion in 2016—the second largest stock of French FDI in Africa after Morocco"[222]. These bilateral relations have helped strengthen the political alliance and benefit growth and employment in both countries.

Notably, the cooperation between the two states has focused on development cooperation in human rights and security. Apart from the Boko Haram terrorist group, the West African region has historically been affected by varying degrees of terror activities, coupled with the rise of the 2012 Tuareg rebellion in northern Mali, which led to a lot of arms finding their way into the civilian population[223]. Nigeria, as a regional leader, has prioritised the issue of combating terrorism in the region. Nigeria considers this type of foreign policy an internal issue since regional conflicts could potentially move into its territory and

---

[222] *France's Regional Economic Service.URL: https://www.diplomatie.gouv.fr/en/country-files/nigeria/france-and-nigeria(accessed on: 07.11.2021).*

affect internal security. In recent times, insecurity in the West African region has increased to unacceptable levels. Insurgents, rebels, militants, and terrorists have threatened the peace and security of West Africa, leading to the loss of lives and massive destruction of properties.

Accordingly, France and Nigeria seek to develop their political relations. In addition to France's support against terrorism in the Lake Chad region, after the Paris Summit in May 2014[224], bilateral relations have been growing, particularly in the sectors of the economy and culture. Nigeria, because of its demographic, economic, cultural, and political importance, has a crucial role in Africa.

Again, Nigeria is France's leading trading partner in sub-Saharan Africa and the fourth-largest in Africa, behind Morocco, Algeria, and Tunisia. In 2019, trade between the two countries amounted to €4.479 billion. In 2018, Nigeria ranked 28th among suppliers to France in the world and was France's 60th-largest customer. Moreover, with an FDI stock of €9.4 billion in 2018, France is one of Nigeria's leading investors.

France also supports the Multinational Joint Task Force (MNJTF) in its fight against Boko Haram through intelligence and operational cooperation and provides political support to the Lake Chad Basin Commission. France is part of the International Support Group for Regional Strategy for the Stabilisation, Recovery, and Resilience of the African Union and the Chad Basin Commission.

**Military Relations**: Security and defence cooperation aims to provide support to Nigeria's army, navy, and police forces. Military cooperation focuses on French language education to provide support to the strategy President Buhari drafted, which aims to ensure in five years that most officers are able to interact with the armed forces of Francophone countries in the subregion. The maritime security project concerns hydrography, diving, maritime cyber security, fleet maintenance, and special forces. This broadens France's cooperation with the Gulf of Guinea's leading navy. Internal security and civil

---

[224] *France Diplomacy. https://www.diplomatie.gouv.fr/en/country-files/nigeria/france-and-nigeria-65149/(accessed on: 07.11.2021)*

protection cooperation focuses on airport security and the fight against drug trafficking.

France also supports the Multinational Joint Task Force (MNJTF) in its fight against Boko Haram through intelligence and operational cooperation, working from N'Djamena. At the political level and concerning development in the Lake Chad region, France is part of the International Support Group for Regional Strategy for the Stabilisation, Recovery, and Resilience of the African Union and the Chad Basin Commission[225].

---

[225]Nigeria and France Relations. France Diplomacy. URL:
https://www.diplomatie.gouv.fr/en/country-files/nigeria/france-and-nigeria-65149
(accessed on 27.11.2023)

# Chapter Four

## Nigeria and the International Community

### 4.1 Nigeria and the United Nations

H istorically, the United Nations was formed in 1945, immediately after the end of World War II, by 51 countries[226] who were committed to maintaining international peace and security, developing friendly relations among nations, and promoting social progress, better living standards, and human rights. The United Nations was instituted in pursuit of the following mandates: (1) to maintain international peace and security; (2) to protect human rights; (3) to uphold international law; and (4) to deliver humanitarian aid and support sustainable development and climate action. However, the negotiations that created the organisation took into account the role played by the major victorious allies in the war[227].

The victory and structure of this organisation necessitated the Security Council, which is the United Nations' most powerful organ because of the power wielded by its members from the time of its creation. The United Nations Security Council is charged with maintaining peace and security between nations (Akpotor et al., 2017). For instance, Chapter VII of the United Nations Charter sets out the UN Security Council's powers to maintain peace. It allows the Council to determine the existence of any threat to the peace, breach of the peace, or act of aggression and to take military and nonmilitary action to restore international peace and security[228].

For emphasis, the United Nations Security Council is composed of 15 members: five permanent members with the veto; the People's Republic of China, France, the Russian Federation, the United

---

[226]*The four African countries that made it to San Francisco: The Kingdom of Egypt, the Ethiopian Empire, the Republic of Liberia and the Union of South Africa, as they were known then.*

[227]*United Nations. Peacebuilding, A to Z Site Index // URL:*
*https://www.un.org/peacebuilding/commission/mandate.(accessed on:06.10.2021)*

[228]*United Nations Charter. United Nations, A to Z Site Index.*

Kingdom, and the United States of America; and ten non-permanent members elected for two-year terms by the General Assembly. However, the Security Council has the power to make compelling decisions about member states[229].

Apparently, Africa is the only continent without a permanent seat on the United Nations Security Council. Its membership is limited only to non-permanent seats on the council. According to an amendment to the council structure of 1963, which entered into force on August 31, 1965[230], Africa shares five non-permanent seats along with the Asian continent. This means that there shall be only two and at most three non-permanent members on the continent in one term. Nigeria tops the list of African countries by the number of times it has been on the Security Council. Nigeria has occupied the United Nations Security Council's non-permanent seats five times as it was in 1966–1967, 1978–1979, 1994–1995, 2010–2011 and 2014–2015[231].

The United Nations Organisation has been successful in achieving its fundamental principles and objectives in the area of peace and security. Directly or indirectly, the organisation had averted the third world war as projected by many scholars and political actors in light of the gap between the First and Second World Wars, as well as the regional and communal conflicts. Nevertheless, organisational structure reform is long overdue, which will promote the democracy of states and consolidate peace and harmony among member states.

**Nigerian adhesion to the UN and its Institutions:** the United Nations occupies a central place in the conduct of Nigeria's diplomacy. This is evidenced by the fact that the first organisation joined by an independent Nigeria was the UN on 7 October 1960[232]. Ever since, Nigeria has appeared to have remained steadfast in its commitment to

---

[229]*United Nations Security Council. Permanent and Non – Permanent Members. A to Z Site Index.*

[230] *United Nations Security Council, Amendment 1963. Agenda 103(a).*

[231]*United Nations Security Council. Non-Permanent Members, Nigeria, A to Z Site Index.*

[232]Ibid

the UN. There were occasional setbacks, most notably the agonising 30-month civil war, which brought Nigeria's statehood under threat when some countries recognised the seceding Biafra, and under the Abacha regime, when Nigeria became a pariah state due to its poor reading of and reaction to unfolding global realities, especially regarding democratisation and human rights. Abacha's attempt to extend his rule challenged the already faltering democratisation process. These actions pushed Western UN member countries, particularly the United States, Great Britain, and Canada, to impose sanctions of various dimensions on Nigeria. For instance, members of the ruling junta and their family members were barred from entering the United States for any reason, including medical attention.

After 62 years of UN membership, to what extent can we say the UN has benefited Nigeria? Nwalie (2020) provides a methodological perspective through which we can answer the question. For him, doing justice to this question requires determining whether or not the participation of Nigeria in the UN has enhanced or hindered the preservation, protection, and promotion of Nigeria's national interests and foreign policy objectives.

In fact, the UN has served Nigeria mainly as an enabler in its pursuit of these interests and objectives. For instance, the UN provided Nigeria with a credible platform for the struggle against colonialism in Africa and white minority rule in South Africa. This was made possible by several UN resolutions against colonialism, especially the 1960 UN General Assembly Resolution 1514 (XV) on the Granting of Independence to Colonial Countries and Peoples[233]. Under the auspices of the UN, Nigeria has participated in more than 15 international peacekeeping operations involving well over 200,000 Nigerians. Through its participation in these operations, the country has garnered relevant military experience in terms of training, exposure to, and use of modern technology. The country has also been able to improve the economic and social well-being of its people as many more Nigerians have gained access to modern medical facilities and health care delivery, pipe-borne water, and education through UN specialised agencies and programmes, e.g. the United Nations

---

[233] *United Nations. Declaration on the Granting of Independence to Colonial Countries and Peoples. 1960General Assembly resolution 1514 (XV).*

Development Programme (UNDP), the United Nations Children's Fund (UNICEF), the World Health Organisation (WHO), and many more.

**Membership Issues in the United Nations Security Council:** the uncommon United Nations constitutional crisis, which was caused by the quest and expectations that some parts of the organisation or organ, such as the UN Security Council, might evolve into something far more effective and powerful than anticipated, thus, it has little or no impact on organisational efficiency as it relates to the maintenance of peace and security, as stipulated in Chapter VII of the UN Charter[234].

The United Nations Charter confirms and endorses a highly differentiated international society, despite the rhetoric of state equality its organisational structure portrayed. Excessive political power is reserved to five of the strongest states by giving them a dominant power and responsibility in the Security Council to bind all the other member states on matter relating to the maintenance of international peace and security, as stipulated in Chapter VII of the UN Charter.

For emphasis, the five members of the UN Security Council have the duty to determine the existence of any threat to the peace, breach of the peace, or act of aggression and further make a recommendation or even decide on what approaches shall be taken in accordance with Articles 41 and 42 to maintain or restore international peace and security.

To buttress this, Leland et al. (1969) found that the concessions given by the major powers were clear enough to justify the activities of the Charter and that the smaller powers hardly succeeded in introducing important changes in the system, like in the Dumbarton Oaks Proposals, which determined the establishment of the international organisation for the maintenance of peace and security, which in turn created the United Nations in 1945.

---

[234] *United Nations Charter, Chapter VII. Peace, Dignity and Equality on Healthy Planet.*

The veto power assigned to each of the five permanent member states remains the only constitutional limitation for other state due to its excessive power. Although the Charter was necessitated from the inception of the organisation in 1945 due to the practices within the UN system, which pave the way for several constitutional controls over Security Council activities, however, the chapter does not incorporate a constitutional theory of checks and balances between separate branches, but the reciprocal operation of the veto during the Cold War and the resultant paralysis of the Security Council created a system that was functionally equivalent (Reisman, 2017).

More importantly, during the Cold War, the General Assembly grew with the admission of many newly independent states, and in the process, many became restive about the Assembly's limited powers as regards the Security Council position. Within the interval, specifically in 1963, in response to the ongoing pressure from the newly enlarged General Assembly, a constitutional reform was carried out, which included an additional four nonpermanent seats to the six already existing seats on the Security Council, making it a total of ten nonpermanent seats[235].

Meanwhile, the General Assembly tries to extend its range of activities into the area of peace and security, which indirectly portrays a threat to the Security Council, but as long as the Security Council remains paralysed, both organs are always in harmony. The paralysis of UN Security Councils served as a justification for judicial activism[236]. Moreover, even when the General Assembly and the Security Council were simultaneously seized of a dispute, the latent constitutional and jurisdictional conflicts receded if, as sometimes occurred, both organs were asked by the same parties to do substantially the same things to synchronise their cooperation (Nwalie 2020).

Other powers conferred on the General Assembly by the Charter include taking action in cases of a threat to the peace, breach of peace, or act of aggression when the Security Council has failed to act owing to the negative vote of a permanent member. In such instances, as

---

[235] *General Assembly Resolutions. 1991 A (XVIII), UN GAOR, 18th Session. GAOR 18th Session, Supplement No. 15 Resolutions and Decisions, at 21, UN Doc. A/5515 (1963).*

[236] *Military and Paramilitary Activities in and Against Nicaragua. Jurisdiction and Admissibility, 1984 ICJ REP. 392, 433, para. 93, Nov. 26,1984.*

stipulated in Uniting for Peace, 377 (v) Resolution of November 1950, the Assembly may consider the matter immediately and recommend collective measures to its members to maintain or restore international peace and security.

Nevertheless, some of the political leaders from the smaller states in the General Assembly have grown up operating in this changing environment to change the status quo. Most of the states aspired, individually, to admission to the most exclusive club and organisation such as BRIC, Shanghai Cooperation Organisation, EU, and AU in the world (Reisman, 2017), to limit or abolish the veto of the Security Council members. Unfortunately, none of these initiatives proved successful due to the political and economic control exercised by the various member states of the Security Council. Despite some irregularities, the Security Council decision remains final.

For instance, the Libyan Arab Jamahiriya suit in the International Court against the United States and the United Kingdom for alleged violations of its rights under Act 14 of 1971, the Montreal Convention[237], was considered an action orchestrated to deceive a government incriminated in state terrorism to evade condemnation and sanction by the Security Council (Reisman, 2017). However, Libya's request for interim measures and the jurisdictional boundary between the International Court and the Security Council proved abortive, and the Court ran into a crisis with world constitutional issues that had been settled over five years ago.

The constitutional crisis between the General Assembly and the Security Council was created due to excessive political power given to Security Council member states and the similarity in the functions of both organs, which are centred on the maintenance of international peace and security, as well as the use of vetoes, by the five Security Council members.

Question of Veto Central to the General Assembly's Debate on Security Council Reform

---

[237]*Montreal Convention of 1971. Convention for the Suppression of Unlawful Acts against the Safety of Civil Aviation No. 14118.*

With increased violent conflicts around the world and heightened scrutiny of the Security Council's actions as a result, the General Assembly met on November 16, 2023, for its annual debate on how to reform the 15-nation organ, with speakers Dennis Francis reiterating their calls to make it more representative, transparent, and accountable in order to address the most serious threats to international peace and security.

Noting that the issue of Security Council reform has been on the Assembly's agenda for 44 years, speakers differed on how to reshape the Security Council, with some delegates highlighting the need for more inclusive and representative membership and others arguing for limiting the use of the veto.

According to the speaker, Dennis Francis, the United Nations seems paralysed largely due to divisions within the Security Council, which is falling dangerously short of its mandate as the primary custodian for the maintenance of international peace and security. Without structural reform, the performance and legitimacy of the Council will continue to suffer, as will the credibility and relevance of the United Nations itself, he said, urging Member States to break through ingrained positions and take practical steps in support of effectiveness and inclusion.

The representative of Saint Vincent and the Grenadines, His Excellency Ralph Gonsalves, speaking for the L.69 group of developing countries from Africa, Latin America and the Caribbean, Asia, and the Pacific, said the overrepresentation of Western countries in the Council does not reflect the geopolitical diversity of the United Nations nor the geopolitical realities of the twenty-first century. "That it is no longer fit for purpose is now a stark reality," he said, adding that reform is not only urgent but a precondition to international peace, stability, and security.

Drawing attention to the underrepresentation of countries on the African continent, the delegate of Sierra Leone, Sulay-Manah Kpukumu, speaking for the African Group, observed that "Africa remains the only major continent without representation in the permanent category of the Security Council and under-represented in the non-permanent category". Africa's demand for two permanent seats—with all the rights and prerogatives of current members, including the right of veto, and two additional non-permanent seats—is a matter of common justice, he stressed.

However, there was broad support for expanding the membership, in both permanent and non-permanent categories, and for unrepresented or underrepresented regions and continents such as Africa and Asia to have a "meaningful seat" at the table[238].

**Nigeria's Aspiration for Security Council Membership**: In the contemporary period, due to the dynamic and complex nature of the international system, Nigeria, among other African states, has called for democratisation and better regional representation in the UN Security Council. The country believes that United Nations reform would encourage its permanent membership at the Security Council. Notwithstanding, the call for 143 n of the United Nations Security Council has been longstanding (Schlesinger, 1997).

Nigeria has been one of the leading African countries fully in support of the demand for a comprehensive reform of the UN Security Council. Nigeria's support stems from both its pan–African focus, especially the collective opportunities such reform might offer Africa and its people, and from its national interest as a potential beneficiary of an enlarged Security Council (Nwalie, 2020). The basic justification for the call for reform revolves around numerous factors, such as changing the international environment in which the UN operates and the need to adapt to the attendant challenges, etc. According to Schlesinger (1997) the reformation of the UN can be done effectively only if certain misconceptions about its origins and its administration can be fully identified and dispelled. He believed that the UN was created for political reasons and remains torn between the manoeuverings of democratic and dictatorial and northern and southern powers. The above–mentioned factors have been transforming the realities of 1945, the fundamental principle by which the UN was established.

---

[238]*UN Meeting Coverage General Assembly Plenary. Seventy-Eighth Session, 34th & 35th Meeting (AM &PM). November 16, 2023.*

It is imperative to note that the United Nations was instituted with 51 nations when the process of colonialism was still at its very peak and the Cold War dominated the agenda of the major powers. However, the colonies were therefore perceived and viewed as a basic instrument of power for the colonial masters, such as Great Britain and France, whom they automatically served to enhance their power ranking and assure a permanent seat on the Security Council (Nwalie, 2022). However, the situation has changed at the moment due to the system of operation and size of the organisation, which have contributed immensely to the democratic value of its member states. For instance, the increase in the number of its memberships to 193 and the veto power given to five permanent members of the Security Council encouraged the maintenance of international peace and security. Again, the completion of the decolonisation process had a significant impact on the structure and membership of the UN.

Apparently, the geographical structure of the organisation has also changed significantly. At the inception of European and American institutions, the termination of colonial rule meant that other regions such as Africa, Asia, Latin America, and the Pacific now constitute a much larger portion of the membership. These changes have been a formidable basis for the call and need for reform of the Security Council to give a sense of belonging and a global character to these other regions (Nwalie, 2020).

Again, the UN's inability to respond quickly to prevent the outbreak and spread of conflict in Rwanda and Sudan, etc., has contributed to the quest for its Council reform. Most scholars have attributed the slow and inadequate responses of the UN to the African trouble spots to Security Council failure, which is probably connected to the use and abuse of veto power conferred on its members. However, other contradictions can also be associated with the internal workings of the UN (Saliu et al., 2008).

For emphasis, the veto power accorded to the five permanent members of the Security Council has been regarded as undemocratic and unrepresentative of the current membership. Thus, the issues of efficiency, transparency, and accountability in the workings and methods of the UN have also been of greater concern. However, it requires a system of devolution of powers to strengthen the General

Assembly and the Secretariat, but not to the detriment of the Security Council.

Subsequently, under Kofi Annan as UN Secretary-General, a proposal by the High-Level Panel (HLP) to redress the imbalance of presentation in the Security Council in fulfilment of General Assembly Resolution 52(2)[239], in conformity with the Millennium Declaration, which stresses the importance of a comprehensive reform of the United Nations (Osuntokun, 2008).

According to the High-Level Panel proposal and recommendations, we suggested two models for the reform of the UN Security Council. Both models suggest the increase in seats on the UN Security Council to redress the question among the regional groups about the composition of the Council. The first model recommends an additional six permanent seats and four non-permanent members in the Security Council, which would increase the Council's membership from 15 to 25.

The six new permanent members would be elected according to the following pattern: two to Africa, two to Asia (Japan and India), one to Europe (Germany), and one to Latin America (Brazil), while the four new non-permanent members would be as follows: one from the African States; one from the Asian States; one from the Eastern European States; and one from Latin American and Caribbean States[240].

Nevertheless, the panel recommended that the General Assembly should elect Security Council members by giving preference to the top three financial contributors to the regular budget of the UN in their relevant regional groups, the top three voluntary contributors, or the top three contributors of troops from their regional areas to the UN peacekeeping operations. In this light, Nigeria could be the most suitable candidate, taking into account its military troops to the UN

---

[239] *General Assembly Resolution. Report of the Secretary-General. Security Council Fifty-second year. A/52/581, S/1997/866, 6 November 1997.*

[240] *Resolution on Security Council Reform, Document A/59/L.64. General Assembly Opens Debate on Group of Four Sponsored Draft Resolution on Security Council Reform. 2005.*

---

and ECOWAS for peacekeeping missions and its huge financial contributions to the UN regular budget, as well as the ECOWAS and AU annual budgets, respectively.

In addition, Nigeria, Algeria, Angola, Egypt, Morocco, and South Africa are the highest voluntary contributors in Africa (Saliu, 2012). Nigeria has contributed the most military troops to the AU/UN peacekeeping mission under the auspices of the ECOWAS-ECOMOG. Nevertheless, the country has maintained the same percentage of financial contributions as Egypt, South Africa, and Algeria in the past few years. *See the Appendix for additional sample items.*

**Below is a Scale of Assessment for AU contributors**

| Member State | Scale of Assessment% for 2014–15 | Scale of Assessment % for 2016–18 | Scale of Assessment % for 2018–19 | Scale of Assessment% for 2020–21 | Scale of Assessment% for 2021–22 |
|---|---|---|---|---|---|
| Algeria | 12.904 | 12.000 | 9.600 | 7.525 | 7.525 |
| Angola | - | - | - | 7.525 | 7.525 |
| Egypt | 12.904 | 12.000 | 9.600 | 7.525 | 7.525 |
| Morocco | - | - | 9.600 | 7.525 | 7.525 |
| Nigeria | 12.904 | 12.000 | 9.600 | 7.525 | 7.525 |
| South Africa | 12.904 | 12.000 | 9.600 | 7.525 | 7.525 |
| | | | | | |
| Tier 1 (above) | 51.61 | 48.000 | 48.000 | 45.151 | 45.151 |

**Table 1. AU scale of assessment as a percentage from the 2014 and 2022 financial years**

The above scale of assessment shows the financial contributions from the top seven AU member states for the following period: 2014 and 2015[241]; 2016 to 2018[242]; 2018 and 2019[243]; 2020 and 2021[244]; 2021 and

[241] *African Union Handbook. Guide for those working with and within the African Union. 2015.URL: https://akb.au.int/displaybitstream?handle=AKB/896. (accessed on: 13.04.2021).*
[242] *African Union Handbook. Guide for those working with and within the African Union. 2017. URL:https://au.int/sites/default/files/pages/31829-file-african-union-handbook-2017-edited.pdf. (accessed on: 13.04.2021).*
[243] *African Union Handbook. Guide for those working with and within the African Union. 2019. URL:*

$2022^{245}$ which are based on the principles of ability to pay, solidarity, and equitable burden-sharing to avoid risk concentration. However, emphasis is laid on Nigeria, Egypt, and South Africa in conformity with the UN High-Level Panel.

In line with this judgment, the African Head of State and Government reached a consensus at their mid-term summit in Abuja, Nigeria, in 2005 by choosing the first model of the proposal submitted by the UN High-Level Panel, which recommends an additional six permanent seats and four non-permanent members in the Security Council that would increase the Security Council membership from 15 to 25.

In preference to the second model, which recommends creating a new category of eight, four–year renewable, term seats and eleven new two–year non–renewable seats divided among the regional groups (Osuntokun, 2008), this position was formally adopted in Addis Ababa on 8 March, 2005, and became the official position of Africa on the reform of the UN Security Council[246].

Finally, the first model of the High–Level Panel draft proposal and recommendations would help to redress the issues among the regional groups on the composition of the Security Council. Moreover, the first model would also attract fairness and equity in the use of veto power[247].

**Assessment of Nigeria's Quest for a Permanent Security Council Seat:** In line with the meeting held by the African Head of State and Government in Addis Ababa on 8 March, 2005, which showed African desire and stance in choosing the first model of the proposal submitted

[244]*African Union Handbook. Arts, Culture and Heritage: Levers for Building the Africa we want. 2021.* URL:*https://au.int/sites/default/files/documents/31829-doc-AU_HBK_2021_-_ENGLISH_web.pdf. (accessed on: 13.04.2021).*

[245] *African Union Handbook. Guide for those working with and within the African Union. 2022.*

[246]*African Union Report on UN Security Council Reform. Audit of the African Union Review High Level Panel.2005.*

[247] *Resolution on Security Council Reform, Document A/59/L.64. General Assembly Opens Debate on Group of Four Sponsored Draft Resolution on Security Council Reform. 2005*

by the UN High–Level Panel, which recommends an additional six permanent seats and four non–permanent members in the Security Council.

This judgment only permits two African states that have contributed hugely to the following aspects: the UN annual regular budget and their regional groups in Africa; UN peacekeeping troops; and the top three voluntary contributors to their regional organisation and the UN. In this regard, there have been three major African contenders who merit the prescribed conditions for qualification. Nigeria, South Africa, and Egypt fall into the category of those who merited the candidature for a UN Security Council permanent member seat as required by the UN High-Level Panel.

Subsequently, Nigeria possesses the criteria that qualify its candidature as one of the two African states to take over the slots melted for Security Council permanent seats in conformity with the proposal and recommendations of the UN High–Level Panel. Nigeria remains the highest contributor from Africa to the UN peacekeeping operations, and its annual regular budget is in accordance with the UN High–Level Panel criteria for Council qualification. For clarity, South Africa has yet to establish a record for global participation in peacekeeping missions, while Egypt is only participating with interest. In other words, its participation has so far been based on discrimination and selectiveness[248].

Nigeria recently contributed the most peacekeeping troops to United Nations peacekeeping operations; in 2013, Nigeria contributed the fifth largest number of peacekeepers to United Nations peacekeeping operations. The United Nations also helped negotiate to adjust the border between Nigeria and Cameroon, resulting in the Greentree Agreement in 2006, which restored peace and harmony[249]. To buttress this, Mbadiwe (2003) said Nigeria's huge contribution to the UN under President Olusegun Obasanjo's administration was to re-integrate the country into the international community to restore the lost glory incurred by his predecessor, Sani Abacha.

---

[248]*UN Department of Public Information. Review of United Nations Peacekeeping. UN Digital Library. 1996.*
[249]*Agreement Transferring Authority over Bakassi Peninsula from Nigeria to Cameroon. UN SG/SM/11745*
*AFR/1737. 2008.*

---

Meanwhile, Nigeria's participation in regional, continental, and international peacekeeping was without discrimination or interest. Nigeria was deeply involved in the struggle for decolonisation in Angola, Mozambique, Namibia, and the struggle against apartheid in South Africa, as well as in the process of creating a name for itself, 'advanced nation', even though it was geographically far from the Southern region of Africa. Nigeria is central to the formation of ECOWAS, restrains the destruction of public order in Liberia, and Sierra Leone, and has contributed hugely to areas such as peacekeeping operations and providing economic incentives for less economically demanding African countries (Saliu, 2012).

According to Gambari (1997), Nigeria's participation in peacekeeping operations was not limited to Africa. He said that more than 200,000 Nigerian troops have participated in the UN peacekeeping operation. For instance, Nigeria has participated in the following peacekeeping missions: United Nations India-Pakistan Observer Mission; United Nations Security Force in West New Guinea; United Nations Interim Force in Lebanon; United Nations Transition Assistance Group Namibia; United Nations Mission for the Referendum in Western Sahara; United Nations Operations in Somalia; United Nations Protection Force; United Nations Assistance Mission in Rwanda; United Nations Groups in the Aouzou Strip; United Nations Iran–Iraq Military Observer Groups (Saliu et al., 2008).

Beyond Nigeria's contributions to the UN peacekeeping missions, another major credential is that Nigeria has served as the Chairman of the UN Special Committee against Apartheid, the main instrument through which the UN engaged in attending to the white minority rule in South Africa. Accordingly, in September 2019, Tijjani Muhammad Bande (Nigeria) emerged as the 74th President of the United Nations General Assembly (Nwalie, 2020).

The Nigerian troops have acquired relevant military experience in terms of training and exposure to the use of modern technology in participation in UN peacekeeping missions. Nigeria's role in the UN and ECOWAS peacekeeping operations has given the country an edge over other contenders, especially South Africa and Egypt[250], as relating to the criteria of the UN High-Level Panel.

**Regional Context Level:** Nigeria, within the regional context, has incontestably emerged as a regional hegemon because of its role in conflict resolution and peacekeeping. Since Nigeria's independence in 1960, the country has declared its readiness, commitment, and intention, making Africa the centrepiece of its foreign policy (Sesay et al., 1988). It could be seen in the assertion made by Prime Minister Tafawa Balewa in his inaugural speech on 7 October 1960 at the Plenary of the 15th Regular Session of the United Nations General Assembly, exactly six days after Nigeria gained independence and became the 99th member of the organisation that Nigeria hoped to work and cooperate with the UN and its member states, especially in matters related to establishing democratic principles and supporting peace (Akpotor, 2017), as well as Nigeria's readiness to render practical, financial, and diplomatic support to the OAU (now the AU) (Olusanya et al., 1986).

On several occasions, Nigeria had to forfeit the goodwill of the Western world in choosing to antagonise their interests by supporting the liberation of Angola, Mozambique, Namibia, and the struggle against apartheid in South Africa, as well as in the process of creating a name for itself, 'advanced nation', even though it was geographically far from the Southern region of Africa. Nigeria restrains the destruction of public order in Liberia and Sierra Leone and has contributed hugely to areas, such as peacekeeping operations and providing economic incentives for less economically demanding African countries (Saliu, 2012).

Furthermore, Nigeria's involvement in African conflict resolution and management has been noticeable and appreciated by regional and intergovernmental organisations, such as the Economic Community of the West African States and the African Union, where it belongs. Since the formation of the Organisation of African Unity (now the African Union), Nigeria has been spearheading conflict resolution and peace management on the African continent (Ebo et al., 1998).

---

[250] *United Nations Report on MDG, Taking Stock of the Global Partnership for Development.*

In this light, Nigeria, through peacekeeping interventions, has contributed to the quelling of internal and international conflict in Africa. Beginning with its participation in the Congo crisis shortly after independence, it has since remained committed to conflict resolution and peace management in Africa. For instance, Nigeria participated in the peacekeeping mission in Tanzania in 1964, in Chad in the 1980s before the United Nations intervention, and in Namibia from 1989 to 1990 (Saliu, 1998), all in connection with conflict resolution.

Subsequently, Nigeria's peacekeeping efforts in the West African subregion are particularly noteworthy, not essentially because of its immense role in the formation of the ECOWAS Monitoring Group (ECOMOG) but also because most of its roles are immense and exceptional. For emphasis, Nigeria contributed greatly to the operational needs of all contingents (approximately 9000 personnel) in ECOMOG peacekeeping missions from 1991 to 1992 (Saliu, 1998). Additionally, Nigeria spent $8 billion on peacekeeping operations in the Liberia and Sierra Leone conflicts before the intervention of the United Nations.

Nigeria's role in peacekeeping operations in its subregion has continued to be manifested in the developmental aspirations of the continent. In particular, the transmutation of OAU to AU shows that Nigeria has been involved at every stage of the project. Again, Nigerian former President Olusegun Obasanjo chaired the AU between 2003 and 2004. The NEPAD initiative has also been enhanced by Nigeria's commitment, and a Nigerian diplomat, Ambassador Aluko Olokun, served as the head of its implementation committee (Akinterinwa et al., 2005). This, among other factors, has been promoting and protecting the integrity and welfare of Nigeria and its neighbours within the context of unity and development (Ogunnubi, 2018). All of this was in tandem and in consonance with Nigeria's first Prime Minister's ideas to be commensurate with Nigeria's name and status as a 'messiah' of the continent (Claude, 1964).

More importantly, given Nigeria's huge contributions to the peacekeeping mission and other developmental areas, such as economics and socioculture in Africa, it may be appropriate to envisage a smooth path for Nigeria in the journey to being elected as one of the two new African representatives on the UN Security Council permanent seat.

Nigeria's involvement at the regional, continental, and global levels, in terms of peacekeeping missions and other aspects, has qualified the country as one of the two new required African representatives on the UN Security Council permanent seat.

Suffice it to say that since Nigeria attained independence, the successive Nigerian presidents have shown much commitment towards promoting African diplomacy as well as representing the good image of Africans within and in diaspora. In line with this judgement, Nigeria remains one of the two new required African representatives on the UN Security Council permanent seat.

However, the Nigerian government must look at the past, evaluate the present, and intensify efforts towards the diversification of the country's economy, wage a serious war against corruption, rejig the security architecture, and invest heavily in education and advanced technology so that Nigeria can have something to present when the time comes for the reform of the UNSC.

## 4.2 Nigeria-EU Relations

The relations between Nigeria and the Europeans Union are guided by the Cotonou Partnership Agreement, which was signed in 2000 for a 20-year period. The agreement entered into force in April 2003 and expired in November 2021[251]. However, the Cotonou Partnership Agreement allows the EU to help strengthen peace and security, economic and regional integration, energy, environmental sustainability, good governance, human rights, climate, change and related topics of political dispensation in African countries. Moreover, the Cotonou Partnership Agreement aimed to address regional integration with developing countries in Africa, the Caribbean, and the Pacific. Unarguably, Nigeria and the European Union are keen on achieving regional development, political dispensation, and economic and trade cooperation (Gbadebo, 2019).

---

[251] *ACP-The Cotonou Agreement. URL:https://ec.europa.eu/europeaid/node/1584. (accessed on: 07.11.2021)*

**Economic Relations**: the European Union has robust trade relations with Nigeria and remains its most important trading partner for oil and non-oil exports. Nigeria is also a key beneficiary of EU Foreign Direct Investment. The EU Delegation is responsible for dialogue with Nigerian and ECOWAS authorities, investors, and civil society on a wide spectrum of matters affecting bilateral, regional, and multilateral trade issues, such as the advocacy of regional and international trade as a tool for development, the identification of bottlenecks to investments, and the promotion of West African economic integration and intra-regional trade through the EU-West Africa Economic Partnership Agreement (EPA). The EPA, when signed, will support West Africa's investment, industrialisation, and diversification objectives (including agriculture), most noticeably through the opening of markets in Europe, while continuing to provide safeguards for West African companies.

Besides the traditional development cooperation with the government, the EU has put in place new instruments of engagement with the private sector aimed at creating jobs, growing an inclusive economy, and generating wealth and prosperity.

**Political Relations**: the Nigeria-EU Ministerial Political Dialogue is one of the provisions of the Cotonou Partnership Agreement under Article 8. The dialogue enables the Minister of Foreign Affairs of Nigeria to engage the EU Delegation to Nigeria and the Heads of Missions of European Union member states in Nigeria annually[252]. The Forum enables the Minister to brief the EU Delegation and Heads of Missions about Nigeria's state of affairs and also affords the EU States' Representatives the opportunity to discuss issues of bilateral or common interest.

But as revealed above, such cooperation has been beneficial to the Nigeria-EU`s long-standing partner for decades (Gbadebo, 2019). Meanwhile, buttressing this assumption, it is submitted that

---

[252]*The Policy Paper of the Ministry of Foreign Affairs, Abuja, Nigeria prepared by the European Affairs Division, 7 March 2019*

"addressing its self-interests also drives the EU's activities in Africa, which has helped a lot of developmental changes in the Nigerian economy".

On socio-political and economic cooperation, for instance, through the European Development Fund (EDF), the EU`s approach to supporting sustainable development in Nigeria through investment currently amounts to €512 million over the period 2014-2020[253]. On this, Nigeria's engagement with the European Union has been incrementally robust as it has been operating under the European Union External Action Service (EEAS) and the acquis, collective legal term for European Union laws, policies, and obligations). The Union has supported Nigeria's democratic governance and assisted its consolidation through capacity building, grants-in-aid, and technical cooperation[254].

In 2008, the EU and Nigeria agreed on a broader political framework known as the EU-Nigeria Joint Way Forward in order to deepen their relationship. The agreement establishes the principles, guidelines, and priority areas for enhanced political dialogue and cooperation in the wider context of the EU's relations with African, Caribbean, and Pacific (ACP) countries.

Areas of mutual interest and concern for intensified dialogue include peace and security, migration, good governance and democracy, human rights, trade, and regional integration, among others. Also included are justice sector reform, support for free and fair elections, and regional cooperation[255].

A ministerial-level dialogue takes place once a year, with other meetings at the senior officials' level happening more frequently. Ad hoc meetings on matters of common interest, including regional, continental, and global issues, can take place when agreed upon between the two parties.

---

[253] *The Evolving EU-Nigeria Social, Economic Alliance // ThisDay, February 21, 2017.*

[254] *The Policy Paper of the Ministry of Foreign Affairs, Abuja, Nigeria prepared by the European Affairs Division, 7 March 2019*

[255] *EU and Nigeria Relations. Delegation of the European Union to the Federal Republic of Nigeria and ECOWAS. URL:https://www.eeas.europa.eu/nigeria/european-union-and-nigeria_en?s=114. (accessed on 27.11.2023)*

## 4.3 Nigeria and the Commonwealth

On attaining independence, Nigeria became a bonafide member of the Commonwealth Relations. Meanwhile, the Ministry of Foreign Affairs and Commonwealth Relations was officially created in 1961, with Prime Minister Tafawa Balewa appointing Jaja Wachuku as the inaugural Minister of Foreign Affairs and Commonwealth Relations. Before Jaja Wachuku's tenure, Prime Minister Tafawa Balewa served as the Foreign Affairs advocate of Nigeria from 1960 to 1961. In 1963, Nigeria became a sovereign state (a republic) under the rubric of the Commonwealth of Nations.

The diplomatic relations between Nigeria and the Commonwealth owed their emergence to Abubakar Tafawa Balewa, the Nigerian Prime Minister during the Nigerian First Republic in 1963–1966. Nigeria's relationship with the Commonwealth since 1963 has been described as a strategic platform for achieving its national interests in line with the Commonwealth's principles and objectives (Olukayode, 2019).

Moreover, Nigeria's diplomatic relations with the Commonwealth deteriorated following the ratification and adoption of the Harare Commonwealth Declaration at the meeting of Commonwealth Heads of Government held in Harare, Zimbabwe, on 20 October 1990, which also coincided with the end of the Cold War in 1990. The Harare Declaration pledges the Commonwealth countries to work to protect and promote the fundamental political values of the Commonwealth, including democracy, the rule of law, fundamental human rights, universal access to education, sustainable development, and the alleviation of poverty (The Commonwealth, 2016)[256]. The treaty also served as a catalyst for new platforms of friendship and cooperation with member states, in line with the Charter of the United Nations (Uhomoibhi, 2008).

Consequent to the above, two years after the official declaration of the Harare Declaration by the Commonwealth Heads of Government

---

[256]*Commonwealth, T. From the archive: Harare declaration sets out fundamental values.TheCommonwealth. 2016.*

at their meeting in 1990, in Harare, Nigeria was at loggerheads with the Commonwealth over non-compliance with the Harare principles (Uhomoibhi, 2008). This crisis came to a head over General Ibrahim Babangida's annulment of the June 12$^{th}$ presidential election. The presidential election was won by Moshood Abiola and was adjudged the freest and fairest general election in Nigeria's political history (Onasanya, 2009). After the annulment, however, General Ibrahim Babangida later handed over an interim government to Ernest Shonekan, which was hijacked by General Sani Abacha on December 1993. Following the cancellation of the polls and the executions of Ken Saro-Wiwa and eight Ogoni activists in the Niger Delta by Abacha in December 1994, Nigeria became a pariah within the international community. The failure of Nigerian military regimes under Generals Ibrahim Babangida and Sani Abacha to handover to a democratically elected government and their continuing poor domestic human rights records compromised Nigeria's African leadership and capacity to fulfill its obligations, under the Harare principles, to "human rights, good government, and democracy" (Uhomoibhi, 2008), to which it was a signatory in 1990 as a Commonwealth nation.

Accordingly, the re-admission and re-activation of Nigeria's membership within the Commonwealth after its democratic transition in 1999 reopened and improved Nigeria's sub-regional influence in Africa as well as its relations with other member states within the Commonwealth. However, the urgent need for Nigeria to regain international recognition and to win the sympathy of its largest international donor encouraged President Olusegun Obasanjo's administration (1999–2007) to cultivate close relations with Britain and attend the Commonwealth Heads of Government Meeting (CHOGM) in 1999. President Olusegun Obasanjo took the chair of the Commonwealth until the Prime Minister of Malta succeeded him in November 2005. Within the African Commonwealth countries, Nigeria has consistently used its regional power to advance its national interests and the Harare Principles. For instance, the cases of the Gambia and Zimbabwe's political impasses remained contemporary developments in Nigeria's efforts towards the actualisation of the Harare principles among the Commonwealth nations. For the Gambia, Nigeria, as a member of the Commonwealth, strongly believes in the promotion of democracy, security, and democracy in Africa.

Similarly, the Nigerian government under President Obasanjo resisted regime changes through a coup d'état in Sao Tome and Principe in 2003. The Nigerian former President Olusegun Obasanjo, who was the chairperson of the Commonwealth at the time of the coup, sent a strong message to the military adventurists to hand over to a democratically elected government (BCC, 2003)[257]. The Nigerian government promised and subsequently achieved the return of Frederique de Menezes to power in 2003 (Ogundiya et al., 2011), a role played in upholding the Harare Declaration towards the promotion and strengthening of democracy across the Commonwealth of Nations. Another instance where the Nigerian government has demonstrated its commitment to the promotion of Commonwealth objectives has been the case of Guinea-Bissau, where the government of Kuma Yala was overthrown in 2012. Although the government of Kuma Yala was not in compliance with the Harare Declaration, which seeks to promote democracy and respect for human rights, Nigeria and other members of the Commonwealth intervened and ensured the immediate commencement of a transition to a democratically elected government in Guinea-Bissau.

## Concluding Remarks

The book comprehensively traces and puts into proper conceptual and historical trajectory the evolution in Nigeria's foreign policy since the Forth Republic; however, it tries to provide a better measure on how to quell its problems. Thus, the analysis allowed us to identify the centrist position of Nigeria in the formation of continental and subregional institutions in Africa, as well as its involvement in the international community and relations with major powers.

In summary, the book encapsulates the main features and tendencies of Nigeria's foreign policy since 1999, which include:

The origin of Nigeria's foreign policy can be traced to the Lyttelton Constitution of 1954, in which the foundation of Nigeria's foreign

---

[257]*BCC (2003, July 17) Sao Tome coup condemned.The BCCNews.*

policy was laid. The Lyttelton period is associated with the devolution of power for foreign affairs from Britain to the Federal Government of Nigeria. Meanwhile, the concept of Nigeria's foreign policy from its concession is termed 'Afrocentrism.' At the initial stage, Nigeria's foreign policy objectives, which were devoted to Africa-oriented policies in the interest of continental unity and the total decolonisation of the African continent, witnessed a setback in their implementations because of the political will of Great Britain and the United States.

The legal basis of Nigeria's foreign policy is a structure that regulates and controls domestic principles and norms in order to communicate with the outside world. It has developed a complex of legal principles and goals for guiding such formal relationships. In order to implement these principles, Nigeria is vigorously involved in the activities of the African Union, the Commonwealth of Nations, the Economic Community of West African States (ECOWAS), the Non-Aligned Movement, and the General Assembly of the United Nations.

Nigeria's foreign policy institutions, such as the Ministry of Foreign Affairs, the National Assembly, the Presidential Advisory Council on IR, and the Nigerian Institute of International Affairs, are designed to handle and promote the goals and objectives of Nigeria's foreign policy to the members of the international system.

Nigeria's Afrocentric foreign policy was consistently centred on uniting and promoting Africa's political, economic, and sociocultural activities. Despite a few dissenting voices on its foreign policy decisions towards Africa, this fact is validated by Nigeria's commitment to the decolonization of Africa and the right of Africans to self-determination.

The Pan-African Movement became a roadmap for the formation of Nigeria's foreign policy. The West African region was the centre of pan-Africanism in Africa. Nigeria, since independence, has walked the path of pan-Africanism and the right of all peoples to self-determination, and its foreign policy is based on its continued survival, security, and well-being, as well as regional, continental, and universal peace and security and the principles of the UN Charter. Pan-Africanism, which influenced their social and political engagements, contributed to the decision-making process in Nigeria.

Nigeria played a crucial role in shaping the final shape of the

Organisation of African Unity (OAU), which was established in 1963, and its subsequent transmutation into the African Union (AU) in 2002. The OAU gave Nigeria a platform to extend its diplomatic reach and shape the outcomes of major events across the continent. Nigeria championed the campaign against colonialism and institutionalised racism in Africa through the multilateral framework of the OAU.

The calls for the transmutation of the Organisation of African Unity (OAU) to the African Union (AU) became inevitable due to the inability of the organisation to maintain its principles and objectives. African states called for the creation of the African Union (AU) at the extraordinary summit in Sirte, Libya, on September 9, 1999. However, the main objective for the transmutation of the Organisation of African Unity to the African Union (AU) was to shift from state-centred to people-centred interests.

More importantly, Nigeria's economic policy and its national interests, which are centred on Africa, have encouraged the country to cooperate with other African states in pursuing African economic initiatives, such as the New Partnership for Africa's Development (NEPAD) economic initiatives. The New Partnership for Africa's Development (NEPAD) is an African-led strategy for economic development and a poverty eradication initiative on the African continent.

The African heads of state and government signed the 50th Anniversary Solemn Declaration during the Golden Jubilee celebrations of the formation of the OAU/AU in May 2013 as an affirmation of their commitment to support Africa's new path for attaining inclusive and sustainable economic growth and development. However, the declaration marked the dedication of Africa towards the attainment of the Pan-African vision of an integrated, prosperous, and peaceful Africa, driven by its citizens, representing a dynamic force in the international arena, and AU Agenda 2063 is the concrete manifestation of how the continent intends to achieve this vision within 50 years from 2013 to 2063.

Over the years, Nigeria has been using its economic diplomacy, such as hard and soft power resources, to protect economic security and attract foreign investment and project power, particularly within

Africa. It is clear that Nigeria's diplomatic behaviour is rooted in its economic diplomacy and prowess, which provide the country with an opportunity to play a subtle hegemonic role on the continent of Africa.

Since the 1960s, Nigeria has built and developed a cordial relationship with all its neighbours namely Benin, Niger, Chad, and Cameroon, as well as other countries in the West African subregion, with most of which it has bilateral agreements. However, there had been a few times when Nigeria and its neighbours had gotten into arguments about borders. In 1983, Nigeria faced a border dispute with Chad, and military action against Chad was even contemplated by the Nigerian government.

This development led to the establishment of the National Boundary Commission (NBC), which was created to resolve boundary challenges emanating from both internal and external boundaries with Nigeria's immediate neighbors. The National Boundary Commission (NBC) has organised several trans-border cooperation workshops, and these workshops have provided a platform to discuss and redress border disputes.

It is a fact of history that Nigeria played a prominent role in the formation of the Economic Community of West African States (ECOWAS) in 1975. The original intention of the community emanates from Article 2 of the Treaty of Lagos, which was aimed to promote, regulate, and develop all fields of economic activities in order to improve the living standard, maintain economic stability, and promote close relations between ECOWAS member states. In our view, Nigeria's participation in West African economic integration attracts political and economic stability in its subregion.

Nigeria's foreign policy during the formative years of ECOWAS was defined by the prevailing circumstances in the region that allowed the kind of foreign policy that was premeditated to respond to the frequent political instabilities across the region because of incessant military coups, religious intolerance, a lack of social and economic development, and the supremacy struggle between Anglophone and Francophone countries in the region due to their historical experience.

However, Nigeria's leadership role in ECOWAS is determined by its financial contribution to ECOWAS and its member states. Nigeria huge contribution to ECOWAS's can be traced to the ECOWAS

Community Levy Agreement, which was adopted in 1996 by the Authority of Heads of State as the major funding for ECOWAS after the initial contribution regime seemed ineffective.

During the formation of the Economic Community of West African States Ceasefire Monitoring Group (ECOMOG), President Ibrahim Babangida was seen to have spearheaded the formation of the group, essentially because of Nigeria's political will to determine and influence its subregion. However, the Nigerian leadership status in West Africa and Africa at large has gotten out of its endowment of human and natural resources, which encouraged Nigeria's manifest destiny to remain more about influence than power.

Finally, Nigeria's foreign policy has been characterised by a focus on Africa and, by extension, West African institutions. Nigeria's relations with the Lake Chad Basin Commission and Gulf of Guinea Commission are necessitated as a result of the following goals: to exercise hegemonic influence in the region; to regulate and control utilisation of the water and other natural resources in the basin; to uphold African unity and independence; and to examine complaints and promote settlement of disputes, with a view to promoting regional economic cooperation and development. Nigeria has a highly respected profile in Africa that is considered emulating various African issues, and that profile has largely been that of an active member of the international community, and a central player in subregional and African affairs.

Nigeria's desire for regional and continental leadership has forced it to strengthen its relationships with major powers, including the United Kingdom, the United States, the People's Republic of China, and the Russian Federation. Since gaining its independence in 1960, Nigeria has maintained strong relations with the United Kingdom, its former colonial master. The United Kingdom (UK) is now one of Nigeria's strongest allies, and as such, its security issues are of great concern to London. Since the establishment of Nigerian diplomatic relations with the United Kingdom on October 1, 1960, Nigeria-UK bilateral relations have been filled with multidimensional content in the political, diplomatic, defense, economic, and social spheres. The political and diplomatic dialogue between the two states is facilitated by their active cooperation through their membership in international organisations.

The bilateral relations between Nigeria and the United States continued to improve, and cooperation on many important foreign policy goals, such as maintaining peace in the region, was excellent. It is estimated that one million Nigerians and Nigerian Americans live, study, and work in the United States, and more than 25,000 Americans live and work in Nigeria. Nigeria is currently the largest US trading partner in sub-Saharan Africa, mainly due to the high export rate of Nigerian oil, which accounts for 8% of US oil imports, which is half the daily oil production in Nigeria. Nigeria is in fifth place in terms of US oil exports. Bilateral trade in 2010 was estimated at more than 34 billion dollars, which is 51% more than in 2009, mainly due to the restoration of world prices for crude oil. Exports from the United States to Nigeria in 2010 exceeded 4 billion US dollars due to crops (wheat and rice), the automotive industry, oil products, and various equipment. In 2010, US imports from Nigeria totaled more than $30 billion, mostly due to oil. In 2022, the two-way trade in goods between the United States and Nigeria totaled over $8.1 billion.

People's Republic of China-Nigeria relations are cordial, and both countries pursue an independent foreign policy of peace. Both countries are partners in economic and trade relations, always trying to achieve mutual benefit and a win-win outcome. Bilateral relations between the People's Republic of China and Nigeria have reached a new height following the trade agreement signed on 18 July, 2019 between the representatives of the two countries. Both countries have been cooperating in multiple areas since they established diplomatic ties. The ties were solidified after the agreement between the Nigeria-China Belt and Road Investment Forum held in Hangzhou, Zhejiang, China.

More importantly, the re-introduction of the Forum on China-Africa Cooperation (FOCAC) summit has brought huge and positive changes to the two countries. This forum was born in 2000 to consolidate and advance Sino-African relations and also create a framework for the development of mutually beneficial, stable, and long-term relationships between China and Africa.

Chinese development assistance in Nigeria has focused on

economic investment and reconstruction, such as in the electric power sector, solid minerals, agriculture, rail transportation, and housing infrastructure.

Nigeria's relationship with Russia began with the Union of Soviet Socialist Republics (USSR) and has lasted ever since. The first major diplomatic cooperation between both nations was during the Nigerian civil war from 1967 to 1970. The Nigerian government turned to the Soviet Union for military cooperation, which eventually led to its victory in the war. Nigeria and Russia have maintained cordial diplomatic, political, economic, and cultural relations.

In October 2019, the President of the Federal Republic of Nigeria, Muhammadu Buhari, and President Vladimir Putin of the Russian Federation reached a new agreement to strengthen Nigeria-Russia relations. They reached a mutual opinion that it is crucial to put Nigeria-Russia relations on a fast track and pursue the completion of partially completed and abandoned projects initiated by both countries. The two leaders agreed to start new infrastructure projects and expand trade and investment, security, and military cooperation.

It is interesting to note that since 2019, after the first Russia-Africa Summit in Sochi, the Nigerian government has hosted several delegates from the Russian business community, taken part in many exhibitions, and is currently experiencing a robust and healthy relationship with the Russian Federation, mostly in the areas of trade and investment. Nigeria has seen a rise in trade volume between both nations. During the last 25 years, the exports of Nigeria to Russia have increased at an annual rate of 6.36%, from $8.3M in 1996 to $38.8M in 2021.

Nigeria's involvement at the international level, essentially at the United Nations, as well as its desire to reposition the African Union at the United Nations, has had a huge impact on African policy. Apparently, Africa is the only continent without a permanent seat on the United Nations Security Council. Its membership is limited only to non-permanent seats on the council. According to an amendment to the council structure of 1963, which entered into force on August 31, 1965, Africa shares five non-permanent seats along with the Asian continent. This means that there shall be only two and at most three non-permanent members on the continent in one term. Although the debate about who represents Africa and whether Africa should obtain a permanent seat or veto power in the Council falls beyond the purview of this book, However, as far as Africa's membership in the Council and the benefits that may accrue from this for the continent are concerned, it is evident that being on the Council affords a country or continent the opportunity to highlight issues it deems important and to bring them to the attention of the world through this body.

In responding to the question, Nigeria posed as the most credible candidate to occupy the position according to the prescribed conditions for qualification or the criteria set by the High-Level Panel (HLP) in the General Assembly. Presently, Nigeria tops the list of African countries by the number of times it has been on the Security Council. At the moment, Nigeria has occupied this position five times, as it did in 1966–1967, 1978–1979, 1994–1995, 2010–2011, and 2014–2015, and is also the highest African contributor. Under the auspices of the UN, Nigeria has participated in more than 15 international peacekeeping operations involving well over 200 000 Nigerians, and for more than 20 years, Nigeria served as the Chairman of the UN Special Committee against Apartheid, the main instrument through which the UN engaged in helping to end white minority rule in South Africa.

Moreover, Nigerian relations with the European Union have been strengthening, particularly in the sectors of the economy, security, and culture. Individually, Nigeria's major bilateral donors within the EU member states are Germany and France. Nigeria receives a series of supports from the French government, such as economic development, security, health, support for the private sector, and agriculture. Currently, the focal point between Nigeria and France is trade and security. Again, French exports to Nigeria consist of refined petroleum products, pharmaceuticals, mechanical, electric, electronic, and computer equipment, and agro-food products, while exports from Nigeria to France are mainly made up of petroleum products.

Meanwhile, Nigeria and Germany have exchanged bilateral relations in various aspects. The cooperation between Germany and Nigeria on migration issues has intensified in recent years. The two countries liaise with one another on the return of Nigerian migrants, and Germany is also assisting the Nigeria Immigration Service (NIS) in the areas of biometric data collection and border management. Nigeria is Germany's second-largest trading partner in sub-Saharan Africa. One priority of bilateral economic relations is cooperation in the energy sector.

In our view, the diplomatic relations between Nigeria and the Commonwealth owed their emergence to Abubakar Tafawa Balewa, the Nigerian Prime Minister during the Nigerian First Republic in 1963–1966. Nigeria's relationship with the Commonwealth since 1963 has been described as a strategic platform for achieving its national interests in line with the Commonwealth principles and objectives.

## Glossary

**Alliance:** a formal agreement between two (bilateral) or more (multilateral) states to cooperate in security matters; a formal security coalition of states with specified commitments.

**Armed conflicts**: is the use of armed force between two or more organised armed groups, governmental or non-governmental alike.

**Ambassador**: is an important, high-ranking official stationed in a foreign country who represents his own country's interests there.

**Balance of power:** is a concept that refers to a condition of or tendency towards equilibrium (or balance) among states.

**Bilateral communications**: are those that directly involve only two countries.

**Bilateral aid**: is the dominant type of state-run aid.

**Bilateral negotiation:** is the process of making offers and counteroffers by the two parties as agents with the aim of finding an acceptable agreement through mobile devices in a mobile commerce environment.

**Bilateral relations**: refer to political, economic, cultural, and historical ties as well as people-to-people contact.

**Bilateral trade:** is the exchange of goods between two nations, promoting trade and investment by reducing and eliminating trade barriers.

**Business networking:** is the process of establishing a mutually beneficial relationship with other businesspeople and potential clients or customers.

**Career diplomats:** are people from any other professional background who may equally be designated by an official government to act as diplomats abroad.

**Ceasefire agreement:** is a temporary stoppage of a war in which each side agrees with the other to suspend aggressive actions.

**Central government:** is the government that has controlling power over a unitary state.

**Chain migration:** is referring to the social process by which migrants from a particular town follow others from that town to a particular destination.

**Civic diplomacy**: involves "people-to-people" contact through all means, involving social media and conventional media (press diplomacy), with particular emphasis on social (humanitarian) and concrete cultural activities.

**Civil authority**: is the practical implementation of a state on behalf of its citizens, other than through military units, that enforces law and order and is used to distinguish between religious authority and secular authority.

**Civil servant:** is a person employed in the public sector by a government department or agency.

**Civil society:** is the "third sector" of society, along with government and business. It comprises civil society organisations and non-governmental organisations.

**Civic organisation:** is any local service club, fraternal society or association, or local civic league or association of 10 or more persons that is not proprietary but operates exclusively for educational and charitable purposes, including the promotion of community welfare, etc.

**Coalition**: is the denotation for a group formed by two or more people, factions, states, political parties, or militaries.

**Coercion**: is the practice of forcing another party to act in an involuntary manner by means of threats or force.

**Colonisation**: is the process of taking control and settling down on a foreign land with little or no regard for the indigenous populations or their land, whose resources are usually exploited for the benefit of the dominant political power.

**Commercial diplomacy**: is diplomacy that focuses on the development of business between two countries.

**Conflict behaviour:** behaviour that results from experiencing two incompatible motivational states at the same time.

**Conflict mediation:** is a process of conflict resolution in which a neutral mediator assists the parties through constructive discussion and negotiation of their issues in order to reach a mutually acceptable resolution.

**Conflict prevention:** is a broad term that refers to a variety of activities and strategies within the field of peacebuilding that are deployed to preempt and subsequently neutralise potential triggers to widespread violent conflict.

**Conflict process**: the development of a conflict through its various stages

**Conflict resolution:** is a way for two or more parties to find a peaceful solution to a disagreement among them.

**Culture:** is an umbrella term that encompasses the social behaviour and norms found in human societies, as well as the knowledge, beliefs, arts, laws, customs, capabilities, and habits of the individuals in these groups.

**Cultural diplomacy**: is a type of public diplomacy and soft power that includes the "exchange of ideas, information, art, language, and other aspects of culture among nations and their peoples in order to foster mutual understanding".

**Cultural identity:** is the sense of belonging to a group.

**Cultural integration**: is when individuals from one culture adopt practices from another culture without diminishing their own.

**Customs union:** is generally defined as a type of trade bloc that is composed of a free trade area with a common external tariff.

**Delegation**: refers to a small group of people, representing a particular country, who have been sent elsewhere to negotiate with other people on behalf of their country or a larger group.

**Democratic governance:** is a system of government where institutions function according to democratic processes and norms, both internally and in their interactions with other institutions.

**Democratisation**: is the transition to a more democratic political regime, including substantive political changes moving in a democratic direction.

**Deregulation**: is the process of removing or reducing state regulations, typically in the economic sphere.

**Diplomacy**: is the management of relationships between countries.

**Diplomat:** an official representing the interests of a particular state or a plenipotentiary international organisation.

**Diplomatic mission:** is a diplomatic representation (more commonly referred to as an embassy) of the sending State (accrediting state) with the host State (receiving state).

**Dispute settlement:** is the process of resolving disputes between parties.

**Domestic policy**: are administrative decisions that are directly related to all issues and activity within a nation's borders.

**Domestic political**: is the set of activities, events, and situations that happen or exist within one particular country.

**Economic autonomy:** is the sense of women's capacity to generate income and personal financial resources based on access to paid work under conditions of equality with men.

**Economic crisis:** is a severe and sudden upset in any part of the economy.

**Economic diplomacy:** is traditionally defined as decision-making, policy-making, and advocating for the sending state's business interests.

**Economic integration:** is an arrangement among nations that typically includes the reduction or elimination of trade barriers and the coordination of monetary and fiscal policies.

**Economic migration**: is the movement of people from one country to another to benefit from greater economic opportunities in the receiving country.

**Economic reform**: refers to deregulation, or at times, a reduction in the size of government, to remove distortions caused by regulations or the presence of government, rather than new or increased regulations or government programmes to reduce distortions caused by market failure.

**Electoral reform:** is a change in electoral systems to improve how public desires are expressed in election results.

**Essence**: the attributes that make an object or substance what it fundamentally is and that it has necessarily.

**Ethnic group:** is a social category of people who identify with each other on the basis of shared attributes that distinguish them from other groups.

**Executive arm:** is the branch of government exercising authority over and holding responsibility for the governance of a state.

**Foreign aid:** is any type of assistance that one country voluntarily transfers to another, which can take the form of a gift, grant, or loan.

**Foreign policy:** refers to its objectives and activities in relation to its interactions with other states, whether bilaterally or through multilateral platforms.

**Foreign investment:** is the investment in domestic companies and assets of another country by a foreign investor.

**Freedom of navigation**: is a principle of customary international law that states that ships flying the flag of any sovereign state shall not suffer interference from other states, apart from the exceptions provided for in international law.

**Free-trade area**: is the region encompassing a trade bloc whose member countries have signed a free trade agreement (FTA).

**Geopolitics**: refers to the way geography affects the politics and relations between different nations.

**Global forces**: are forces that affect our economy, travel, exchange of goods and services, access to information, communication, health provision, education delivery, etc.

**Global security:** is a term which refers to the measures taken by states and international organisations, such as the United Nations, European Union, and others, to ensure mutual survival and safety.

**Great power**: is a sovereign state that is recognised as having the ability and expertise to exert its influence on a global scale.

**Hard power:** is a form of political power associated with the use of military or economic coercion to correct the behaviour or interests of other political forces.

**Hegemonic influence:** is an influence or control over another country or a group of people.

**Hegemonic status** is a status bestowed by others and rests on their recognition.

**History:** is the study of the past.

**Homegrown terrorism**: is a form of terrorism in which victims "within a country are targeted by a perpetrator with the same citizenship" as the victims.

**Human behaviour**: refers to the way humans act and interact.

**Human factors:** are the study of the interrelationship between humans, the tools and equipment they use in the workplace, and the environment in which they work.

**Human rights:** are moral principles or norms that describe certain standards of human behaviour and are regularly protected in municipal and international law.

**Humanitarian aid**: is material and logistical assistance to people who need it.

**Humanitarian intervention**: a state's use of military force against another state, with stating that its goal is to end human rights violations in that state.

**Humanitarian work:** requires being responsible, conscious of the circumstances of other people's lives, and helping them on the basis of need without discrimination.

**Intra-community trade:** refers solely to the movement of animal products between EU Member States.

**Inter-governmental organisations:** is an organisatio composed primarily of sovereign states.

**Interregional migration:** –is the permanent movement from one region of a country to another.

**Internal security:** is the act of keeping peace within the borders of a sovereign state or other self-governing territories.

**International cooperation:** is the interaction of persons or groups of persons representing various nations in the pursuit of a common goal or interest.

**International humanitarian law:** is a set of rules which seek, for humanitarian reasons, to limit the effects of armed conflict.

**International migration:** occurs when people cross state borders and stay in the host state for a certain minimum period of time.

**International norms:** are the product of the foreign policies of states and other actors.

**International Policy:** is a think tank based in DC that strives to make peace, justice, and sustainability the central pursuit of US foreign policy.

**International relations:** is the study of the relations of states with each other, with international organisations and with certain subnational entities.

**International system:** is the global constellation of states.

**International trade:** is the exchange of capital, goods, and services across international borders.

**Leadership style**: refers to a leader's characteristic behaviours when directing, motivating, guiding, and managing groups of people.

**Legislative arm**: is a deliberative assembly with the authority to make laws for a political entity such as a country or city.

**Legitimate authority**: is one that is entitled to have its decisions and rules accepted and followed by others.

**Legitimate power**: is power you derive from your formal position or office held in the organisation's hierarchy of authority.

**Middle power**: is a sovereign state that is neither a great power nor a superpower but still has large or moderate influence and international recognition.

**Multilateral aid:** is assistance provided by governments to international organisations like the United

**Multilateralism:** is the process of organising relations between groups of three or more states.

**Multinational corporation**: is usually a large corporation incorporated in one country that produces or sells goods or services in various countries.

**Multilateral institution:** are organisations formed between three or more nations to work on issues that relate to all of the countries in the organisation.

**Multilateral negotiation:** are characterised by intensive international discussions that involve multiple actors.

**Multipolar system:** is a system in which power is distributed at least among three significant poles, concentrating wealth.

**National Affairs:** is a journal of essays covering domestic policy, political economy, society, culture, and political thought.

**National economy:** is the economy of a nation as a whole that is an economic unit and is usually held to have a unique existence greater than the sum of the individual units within it.

**National identity:** is a person's identity or sense of belonging to one state or to one nation.

**Nationalist movement:** is a social and political movement for obtaining and maintaining national identity and autonomy among a group of people.

**National reconciliation:** is the term used for the establishment of so-called 'national unity' in countries beset with political problems.

**National security:** is the security and defence of a nation-state, including its citizens, economy, and institutions, which is regarded as a duty of government.

**Non-governmental organisation:** is a non-profit group that functions independently of any government.

**Non-state actor:** an integral part of global governance.

**Oligopoly:** is a market structure with a small number of firms, none of which can keep the others from having significant influence.

**Open diplomacy:** information sharing at all levels and by all parties is optimal in peacetime.

**Peacebuilding:** efforts aim to manage, mitigate, resolve, and transform central aspects of the conflict through official diplomacy, informal dialogue, negotiation, and mediation.

**Peace enforcement:** is the use of military force to compel peace in a conflict, generally against the will of combatants.

**Peacekeeping:** comprises activities intended to create conditions that favour lasting peace.

**Peacekeeping forces:** are contributed by member states on a voluntary basis.

**Peace maintenance:** is to enable a local population to choose its future development between conditions of violence and calm.

**Peacekeeping operation:** are called upon not only to maintain peace and security but also to facilitate the political process, protect civilians, etc.

**Peace process:** is the set of sociopolitical negotiations, agreements, and actions that aim to solve a specific armed conflict.

**Peace treaty:** is an agreement between two or more hostile parties, usually countries or governments that formally ends a state of war between the parties.

**Peaceful revolution:** is an overthrow of a government that occurs without violence.

**Political actor:** are individuals who are in charge of government institutions, e.g., the foreign ministry, and are considered important policymakers.

**Political association-** is a citizens' association intended to assist in the development of democratic life and the country's political culture, as well as to create a better informed public opinion.

**Political authority:** is the power held by a political entity to require action and claim obedience to its rules.

**Political autonomy:** is the property of having one's decisions respected, honoured, and heeded within a political context.

**Political boundary:** is an imaginary line separating one political unit, such as a country or state, from another.

**Political competition:** is a game between political parties in which each party announces a multidimensional policy vector.

**Political crisis:** is a difficult transitional state of any social system, expressed in a break in its activity.

**Political elite:** is a set of people holding high leadership positions in government, a union of states.

**Political entities:** are basically systems of governing authority organised as governmental power structures.

**Political independent:** is variously defined as a voter who votes for candidates on issues rather than on the basis of a political ideology or partisanship.

**Political integration:** is the integration of components within political systems; the integration of political systems with economic, social, etc.

**Political marginalisation:** a group's relevance, in turn, dictates their political exclusion and discrimination, which are widely believed to underlie economic marginalisation.

**Political migration:** is any migration motivated primarily by political interests.

**Political Reform:** is a programme works towards an open, fair democratic process with equitable opportunities for full participation in order to restore dynamism and growth to the American economy and society.

**Political revolution:** is an upheaval in which the government is replaced or the form of government altered, but property relations are predominantly left intact.

**Refugee crisis:** refers to difficulties and dangerous situations in the reception of large groups of forcibly displaced persons.

**Regionalisation:** can be conceived as the growth of societal integration within a given region

**Regional autonomy**: is decentralisation of governance to outlying regions.

**Regional economics**: is a sub-discipline of economics and is often regarded as one of the fields of the social sciences.

**Regional hegemony:** is the hegemony of one independently powerful state over other neighboring countries.

**Regional interference**: is the most significant obstacle to a sustainable peace and prosperous future in a conflicting state.

**Regional integration:** is the process by which two or more nation-states agree to cooperate and work closely together to achieve peace, stability, and wealth.

**Religious organiation:** is the complex of institutionalised roles and procedures that regulate the relations of men with the supernatural order, however such an order may be conceived.

**Regional power:** is a term used for a state that has power within a geographic region.

**Regional policy:** is the government's policy to boost economic activity in a specific region of the country.

**Regional trade:** is a treaty between two or more governments that defines the rules of trade for all signatories.

**Religious terrorism:** is a type of religious violence where terrorism is used as a tactic to achieve religious goals or is influenced by religious identity.

**Resource scarcity:** is a situation where demand for a natural resource exceeds supply, leading to a decline in available resources.

**Secession agitation:** is the withdrawal of a group from a larger entity, especially a political entity.

**Separatism:** is the advocacy of a state of cultural, ethnic, tribal, religious, racial, governmental, or gender separation from the larger group.

**Security dilemma:** is the core assumption of defensive realism.

**Sectarian violence**: is a form of communal violence that is inspired by sectarianism.

**Shuttle diplomacy:** is the action of an outside party in serving as an intermediary between (or among) principals in a dispute without direct principal-to-principal contact.

**Soft power:** the use of a country's cultural and economic influence to persuade other countries to do something, rather than the use of military power.

**Social behaviour:** is behaviour among two or more organisms within the same species and encompasses any behaviour in which one member affects the other.

**Social marginalisation:** is the social disadvantage and relegation to the fringe of society.

**Social migration**: is moving somewhere for a better quality of life or to be closer to family or friends.

**Social norms:** are the unwritten rules of behaviour that are considered acceptable in a group or society.

**Social organisation:** is a pattern of relationships between and among individuals and social groups.

**Social power:** is a form of power that is found in society and within politics.

**Social values**: are a set of principles that are morally acceptable to society.

**State actor:** is a person who is acting on behalf of a governmental body

**State anarchy:** is the state of a society being freely constituted without authorities or a governing body.

**Statecraft**: is the art of conducting state affairs.

**Superpower:** is a state with a dominant position characterised by its extensive ability to exert influence or project power on a global scale.

**Technical aid:** is a form of aid given to less-developed countries by international organisations such as the United Nations (UN) and its agencies, individual governments, foundations, and philanthropic institutions.

**Trade relations:** contribute to the mutual well-being of participants when each has something the other wants, even in the absence of other elaborating behaviours.

**Transnational corporation**: is an enterprise that is involved with the international production of goods or services, foreign investments, or income and asset management in more than one country.

**Unilateral decision**: is a decision taken by an involved country without the agreement of the other parties involved.

**Unilateral ceasefire**: is a cessation of hostilities, such as in a war that is only binding on one of the combatant sides.

**Veto power**: refers to the power of the five permanent members of the UN Security Council to veto any "substantive" resolution.

# Bibliography

## *Archival Material*

1.ECOWAS SMC Decision A/DEC. 1/8/90, On the Cease – Fire and Establishment of an ECOWAS Cease – Fire Monitoring Group for Liberia, 21 O.J. ECOWAS Spec. Supp. 6. 1992.

2. Protocol of Non – Aggression. ECOWAS Commission, Mediation Guidelines Adopted on 22 April 1978 in Lagos, Nigeria.

3. Revised Treaty of the Economic Community of West African States. Treaties / Agreements / Charters / Protocols / Conventions / Declarations.1993.

4. Supplementary Protocol on the Code of Conduct for the Implementation of the Protocol on Free Movement of Persons, the Right of Residence, and Establishment. 1985.

5. Supplementary Protocol A/P.1/5/79 relating to Free Movement of Persons, Residence, and Establishment. 1979.

6. Supplementary Protocol A/SP.2/5/90 on the implementation of the Third Phase, Right to Establishment of the Protocol on Free Movement. Right of Residence and Establishment.1990.

7. The Agreement on Cessation of Hostilities and Peaceful Settlement of Conflict between the Armed Forces of Liberia, The National Patriotic Front of Liberia, and the Independent National Patriotic Front of Liberia.

8. The Agreement on Transborder Security Cooperation. Cameroon, Nigeria Agree to Bolster Cooperation against Transborder Terrorism. 2012.

9. The Agreement Transferring Authority over Bekasi Peninsula from Nigeria to Cameroon. UN SG/SM/11745 AFR/1737. 2008.

10. The Agreement of Understanding and Treaties Between Nigeria and other countries. Office of the Secretary to the Government of the Federation, Nigeria. May 2, 2013.

11. The Arthur Richards Constitution of 1946.

12. The Bill for an Act to Provide Measures to Combat Terrorism and for Other Related Matters. 2011.

13. The Casablanca Group Treaty of 1961 // DBpedia.

14. The Charter of Organization of African Unity, 1963.

15. The Constitution of the Federal Republic of Nigeria 1979 // ConstitutionNet.
16. The Constitution of the Federal Republic of Nigeria 1963 // ConstitutionNet.
17. The Constitution of the Federal Republic of Nigeria: Extraordinary. 29 (76). 1989. Promulgation Decree No 12. 1989.
18. The Constitution of the Federal Republic of Nigeria, 1999.
19. The Convention on the Rights of the Child. General Assembly resolution 44/25 of 20 November 1989.
20. The Convention and statutes relating to the development of the Chad basin. Signed at Fort Lamy, on 22 May 1964.
21. The Convention A/P.5/582 for Mutual Administrative Assistance in Customs Matters. Cotonou.1982.
22. The Convention for the Suppression of Unlawful Acts against the Safety of Civil Aviation No. 14118.
23. The Constitutive Act of AU.
24. The Convention Creating the Niger Basin Authority. 1980.
25. The Federal Republic of Nigeria 1999 Constitution (as amended) with the National Industrial Court. 98 (20). Government Notice No.103, Official Gazette, The Federal Government Printer, Lagos, FGP 027/32011/2, 200 (OL13).
26. The Hugh Clifford Constitution of 1922
27. The John Macpherson Constitution of 1951.
28. The Monrovia Group Treaty of 1961.
30. The Nigerian Constitution Order in Council. 1954. with the Supplement to Official Gazette. 1960.
31. The Nigerian Constitution of 1999 with Amendments through 2011. Constituteproject.org.
32. The Nigeria Independence Act, 1960 8 & 9 Eliz.2 CH.55.
33. The Oliver Lyttleton Constitution of 1954.
34. The Peace Agreement Between the Government of Sierra Leone and the Revolutionary United Front of Sierra Leone.
35. The Treaty Establishing the Economic Community of West African States Lagos, May 1975.
36. The United Nations Charter. 1945.

37. The Treaty Establishing the African Economic Community of 1991.
38. The Treaty of the Gulf of Guinea Commission.2001.

## Books and Articles

1. Abdullahi Shehu Gusau. Littering the Landscape: An Analysis of the Role of Nigeria in the Transition of OAU to the AU // European Scientific Journal. 2013.
2. Abolade Adeniji. Power and Representations at the United Nations: A Critique of Nigeria's Bid for Permanent Seat in the Security Council // India Quarterly: A Journal of International Affairs. 2005.
3. Adeniyi O. Power, Politics and death A front-row account of Nigeria under the Late President Umaru Musa Yar'Adua, Lagos // International Journal of Research and Innovation in Social Science. 2011.
4. Adeniji A. Power and Representation at the United Nations: a Critique of Nigeria's bid for Permanent Seat in the Security Council. Olusola Ogunnubi & Ufo Okeke-Uzodike. Can Nigeria be Africa's hegemon? // African Security Review. 2016.
5. Adeboye F.I. The Liberian Conflict and the ECOMOG Operation: A Review of Nigeria's Key Contributions // Global Journal of Political Science and Administration. 2020.
6. Adedoyin J. Omede. Nigeria's Relations with Her Neighbours. Studies of Tribes Tribals. 2006.
7. Adibe Clement E. The Liberian Conflict and the ECOWAS & UN Partnership // Third World Quarterly. 1997.
8. Afolabi Gbadebo. The Impact of Afrocentrism upon Nigeria's Foreign Policy: Since Attainment of Independence to the Present Day // European Journal of Humanities and Social Sciences. 2019.
9. Afolabi Gbadebo. Analysis of Nigeria's foreign policy with the European Union, France and Germany: A narrative//international relations. 2019.
9. Afolabi Gbadebo The main priorities of the foreign policy of the Federal Republic of Nigeria: 1976 – 2020: Candidate of Historical Sciences. 2020. [In Russian].

10. Agbegunrin O. Nigerian Foreign Policy Under Military Rule, 1966 –1999 // Westport, Connecticut, and London: Praeger. 2003.
11. Ahmed Mansur & Bokeriya Svetlana. Mandates in the Success of a Peacekeeping Mission: A case study of Liberia // Asia and Africa Today. 2018. [In Russian].
12. Ajaebili C.N. & Oyewole A.N. The option of Economic Diplomacy in Nigeria's Foreign Policy // International Journal of Humanities and Social Sciences. 2011.
13. Aluede Jackson A. Border Relations in Africa and the Impact on Nation Building: A Study of Nigeria and Her Limitrophe Neighbours since the 1960s // African Journal of Governance and Development. 2017.
14. Akindele R.A. (ed.). The Structure and Processes of Foreign Policy Making and Implementation in Nigeria, 1960 – 1990 // Lagos: Nigerian Institute of International Affairs. 1990.
15. Akinyemi A.B. Doctrine of Reciprocity in Nigerian Foreign Policy // Nigerian Institute of International Affairs. 1987.
16. Akinyemi O. Borders in Nigeria's Relations with Cameroon // Journal Arts Humanities. 2014.
17. Akpotor A.S. & Agbebaku P.E. The United Nations Reforms and Nigeria's Quest for a Permanent Seat // Journal of Social Sciences. 2017.
18. Aworawo Friday. Nigeria and ECOWAS since 1999: Continuity and Change in Multilateralism and Conflict Resolution // Journal of African Studies. 2016.
19. Ayoade J.A.A (Eds). The Jonathan Presidency: The Sophomore Year // Ibadan: John Archers Limited. 2014.
20. Bach C.D. Nigeria's Manifest Destiny in West Africa: Dominance with Power // Africa Spectrum. 2007.
21. Bashir S Ibrahim. Cross Border Trade in West Africa: An Assessment of Nigeria and Niger Republic // African Review. 2015.
22. Belov V.A. et al. colonial heritage and Anglophone problem in Cameroon: Africa: regional identity and tradition: annual – 2021 = Apostille: Apostille - 2021- Moscow: RUDN, 255. [In Russian].

23. Bhaso Ndzendze & David Monyae. China's Belt and Road Initiative: linkages with the African Union's Agenda 2063 in Historical Perspective // Transnational Corporations Review. 2019.

24. Charles B. Azgaku. The Role of Nigeria in Peacekeeping Operation in West Africa: 1960 – 2010 // Research on Humanities and Social Sciences. 2015.

25. Chidozie F., Ibietan J. & Ujara E. Foreign Policy, International Image, and National Transformation: A Historical Perspective // International Journal of Innovative Sciences & Humanities Research. 2014.

26. Clement Adibe E. The Liberian Conflict and the ECOWAS & UN Partnership // Third World Quarterly. 1997.

27. Claude S. Phillips. Development of Nigerian Foreign Policy // The Journal of Modern African Studies. 1964.

28. Cyril I. O. Nigeria's foreign policy and transnational security challenges in West Africa // Journal of Contemporary African Studies. 2008.

29. Cyril I.O. Economic Community of West African States on the Ground: Comparing Peacekeeping in Liberia, Sierra Leone, Guinea Bissau, and Côte D'Ivoire // Regional Organizations in African Security Journal. 2009.

30. Dauda M., Mohammad Z. & Mohammad F. Nigeria's Role and Its Peacekeeping Challenges in Africa: An Assessment // European Journal of Social Sciences Studies. 2017.

31. Denisova T.S. Political Conflicts in African countries. Moscow: Vostok, 2010. [In Russian].

32. Denisova T.S. ECOWAS and the problems of regional peacekeeping. On the 40th anniversary of ECOWAS //Asia and Africa today. 2015. [In Russian]

33. Denisova T. M. Tropical Africa: The Evolution of Political Leadership // Institute of Africa of the Russian Academy of Sciences. 2016. [In Russian]

34. Ebenezer E.L. & Opeyemi I.A. Nigerian Foreign Policy: a Fourth Republic Diplomatic Escapade // Journal of Siberian Federal University. Humanities & Social Sciences. 2016.

35. Ebegbulem J. C. The Evolution of Nigeria's Foreign Policy: From

the Pre – Independence and Post – Independence Perspectives // International Journal of Research in Humanities and Social Studies. 2019.

36. Ebegbulem J. C. An Evaluation of Nigeria and South Africa Bilateral Relations // Journal of International Relations and Foreign Policy. 2013.

37. Efem N. Ubi & et al. Nigerian Foreign Policy and Economic Development, 1999-2013 // International Area Studies Review. 2014.

38. Ejitu N. & Chinyere S. Nigerian Foreign Policy and the Democratic Experiment // International Journal of Applied and Advanced Scientific Research. 2016.

39. Eunice N. Sahle. Democracy Constitutionalism and Politics in Africa // Contemporary African Political Economy. 2017.

40. Korendyasov E. Russia Returns to Africa. Africa`s Growing Role in World Politics // Institute for African Studies, Russian Academy of Sciences. 2014. [In Russian].

41. Fafowora O.O. Lest I forget Memoirs of a Nigerian Career Diplomat, Lagos // The Nigerian Institute of International Affairs. 2013.

42. Fawole W.A. (ed.). Nigeria's External Relation and Foreign Policy Under Military Rule, 1966 –1999 // Ile-Ife: Obafemi Awolowo University Press Limited. 2003.

43. Filippov V.R. The African policy of Paris during the pandemic // Institute of Africa of the Russian Academy of Sciences. 2020. [In Russian]

44. Folarin Sheriff. Democratizing the Nigerian Foreign Policy Process: An Inquest for Recipes // EBSU Journal of Society. 2011.

45. Gani J.Y. ECOMOG and West African Regional Security: A Nigerian Perspective // African Issues. 1993.

46. George O.O. From Rookie to Mandarin The Memoirs of a Second-Generation Diplomat, Ibadan: Bolytag International Publishers. 2010.

47. Gill R.S. & Law D. Global Hegemony and Structural Power of Capital // International Studies Quarterly. 1989.

48. Gromoglasova E.S. The Use of Force in Modern Counter-Terrorism: International Legal and Political Aspects, Vestnik RUDN, International Relations, 2016. [In Russian]

49. Ilisan Remo (ed.). The Impact of Terrorism on Education: The North-Eastern Nigerian Experience. // Journal of International Politics and Development. 2016.

50. Imoukhede B.K. Repositioning Nigeria Foreign Policy for National Development: Issues, Challenges and Policy Options // Afro Asian Journal of Social Sciences. 2016.

51. Jenkins Peter A. The Economic Community of West African States and the Regional use of Force // Denver Journal of International Law & Policy. 2008.

52. Khudaykulova A.V. Third World Security Theories // Vestnik RUDN. International Relations. 2016.[In Russian]

53. Kiseleva V.P. Africa Integration and Problems of Foreign Economic Activity. M. 1972. [In Russian]

54. Kosukhin Nikolay D. Political power and the political process in Africa // Bulletin of the RUDN, Ser. Political science.2001. [In Russian].

55. Kostyunina G.M. Integration Processes in Africa: History and the Modern Stage. Russian Foreign Economic Bulletin. 2016. [In Russian]

56. Langley Winston E. (ed.). The Changing Nigerian Foreign Policy // Journal-World Affairs. 1973.

57. Mantzikos Ioannis. The absence of the state in Northern Nigeria: The case of Boko Haram // African Renaissance. 2010.

58. Mbadiwe H. Nigeria Foreign Relation in Obasanjo-Atiku Years. In Chika Oguonu. Nigeria and the NU // African Renaissance. 2006.

59. Miller J. Global Nollywood: The Nigerian Movie Industry and Alternative Global Networks in Production and Distribution // Global Media and Communication. 2012.

60. Murithi T. Problematic Power: The Debate about Nigerian Foreign Policy in the 1980s // Journal of International Studies. 1983.

61. Murithi T. The African Union: Pan-Africanism, Peacebuilding and Development. Routledge. 2005.

62. Nigusie Kassaye W. Michael. Emperor Haile Selassie (I) and the

Organization of African Unity (Devoted to the 50th anniversary of the African Union). Moscow: Vestnik RUDN, World History. 2013. [In Russian].

63. Nigusie Kassaye W. Michael. Haile Selassie I Emperor of Ethiopia. Moscow: RUDN. 2016. [In Russian].

64. Nurudeen O.M. (ed.). Elite Perceptions and Nigeria's Foreign Policy Process // Alternatives Turkish Journal of International Relations. 2014.

65. Nwalie George A.(ed.). African institutional system: Nigerian foreign policy institutions on African //Almanac Cossacks. 2022. [In Russian]

66. Nwalie George A. (ed.). The Question of African Leadership: Nigeria in Focus // International Relations.2022.

67. Nwalie George A. Nigeria Role in the Leadership of Africa: Perspective of International Relations // Academia.edu. 2020.

68. Nwalie George A. Nigeria Political Leadership Strategy in West Africa 1960 – 2019. Moscow: Vestnik RUDN, Global Security and Development Cooperation. 2020.

69. Nwalie George A. Nigerian Multilateral Diplomacy: Case Study of Nigeria's Aspiration for United Nations Security Council Reform // Journal of Language and Linguistic Studies. 2022.

70. Nwalie George A. Separatism and Secession in Nigeria: a case study of Biafra Agitation for Sovereignty between 2000 and 2019 // Institute for African Studies of the Russian Academy of Sciences. 2020.

71. Nwalie George A. & Egesi B. Nigeria – Russia Relations: A Comparative Critical Review // Ethnosocium and International Culture. 2021.

72. Nwalie George A. (eds.). Security situation in sub-Saharan Africa: a study proliferation of small arms and light weapons // Nauka Segodnya Publishing House, 2022. [In Russian]

73. Nwalie George A. Nigeria's Sub - Regional Diplomacy: Nigeria's role in promoting West African Institutions // International Relations. 2023.

74. Nwalie George A. The Question of African Leadership: Nigeria in Focus // International Relations. 2022.

75. Nwalie George A. (eds.). 45 Years of Academic Publication on the Economic Community of West African States: A Bibliographic Analysis // Journal of African Union Studies. 2023.

76. Odubajo T. Domestic Environmental Variables and Foreign Policy Articulation of the Buhari Administration in Nigeria's Fourth Republic // Brazilian Journal of Strategy and International Relations. 2017.

77. Ogilvie A. (ed.). Water, Agriculture, and Poverty in the Niger River basin // Water International. 2010.

78. Ogunbadejo O. Nigeria's Foreign Policy under Military Rule 1966-1979 // Periodical International Journal. 1880.

79. Ogundiya, I. (eds.). AnAssessment of Democratic Trends in Nigeria // New Delhi: Gyan Publishing House. 2011.

80. Oguntade P.G and Abiodun B.J. The Impact of Climate Change on the Niger Basin Hydro-climatology West Africa // Journal Climate Dynamics. 2012.

81. Ogunnubi Olusola (ed.). Can Nigeria be Africa's hegemon? // African Security Review. 2016.

82. Ojakorotu Victor (ed.). Nigeria and Conflict Resolution in the Sub-regional West Africa: The Quest for a Regional Hegemon // African Studies Association of India. 2017.

83. Okeke Vincent O.S. Citizen-Centric Diplomacy: The Challenges for Nigeria's Defence and Security in the 21st Century // International Affairs and Global Strategy. 2014.

84. Okoro U. Victor (ed.). Afro-centrism as the centerpiece of Nigeria's foreign policy: A historical misnomer in the aftermath of xenophobic attacks in South Africa // Cogent Arts & Humanities. 2020.

85. Okeke Vincent O.S. Citizen-Centric Diplomacy: The Challenges for Nigeria's Defence and Security in the 21st Century // International Affairs and Global Strategy. 2014.

86. Olatunde J.B. Nigeria and the Formation of ECOWAS // International Organization. 1980.

87. Olajide Aluko. The New Nigerian Foreign Policy: Developments Since the Downfall of General Gowon // The Commonwealth Journal of International Affairs. 1976.

88 Olukayode Bakare. The Nigerian-Commonwealth and UN

Relations: Nigeria, from Pariah State to Exporter of Democracy Since 1999 // Cogent Social Sciences. 2019.

89. Oluyemi O. Fayomi (ed.). Nigeria's National Image and Her Foreign Policy: An Exploratory Approach // Open Journal of Political Science. 2015.

90. Oluyemi O. Fayomi (ed.). Nigeria's National Image and Her Foreign Policy: An Exploratory Approach // Open Journal of Political Science. 2015.

91. Oke Chris I. (ed.). Diplomatic Shuttles in Foreign Policy: were Obasanjo Tripsduring his Tenure of any benefits to Nigeria // Journal of Social and Management Sciences. 2017.

92. Omotuyi, S. Russo/Nigerian Relations in the Context of Counterinsurgency Operation in Nigeria. Jadavpur Journal of International Relations. 2018.

93. Oshewolo Segun. Rhetoric and Praxis: Nigeria's Africa Diplomacy and the Shaping of the African Union // The Commonwealth Journal of International Affairs. 2019.

94. Oshewolo S. Bringing back the issues: Nigeria's Afrocentric Policy Under President Olusegun Obasanjo // Journal of Commonwealth & Comparative Politics. 2019.

95. Osita Agbu. Cameroon- Nigeria Relations: Trends and Prospectives // Rowman & Littlefield. 2022.

96. Oyeleye Oyediran (Eds). Nigerian Government and Politics under Military Rule. 1966 – 1979 // American Political Science Review. 1980.

97. Pantserev K. A. The States of Sub-Saharan Africa on the way to the Global Information Society // Journal on Systemics, Cybernetics and Informatics. 2010.[In Russian].

98. Pine A. Nigerian Foreign Policy, 1960-2011. Modern Ghana News, an Internet Publication. 2011.

99. Pine A. Pan – Africanism and Nigeria's Foreign Policy: Some Contemporary Notes. Modern Ghana News, an Internet Publication. 2020.

100. Reisman Michael W. The Constitutional Crisis in the United Nation // American Journal of International Law. 1993.

101. Saliu H.A. Review of Debate on Nigeria's Economic Diplomacy // Journal of African Research & Development. 1997/98.

102. Saliu A.H. & Shola Omotola J. Can Nigeria get a UN Security Council seat? // South African Journal of International Affairs. 2008.

103. Saliu A.H. Nigeria's Role Since the Formation of Africa Union: Its Leadership Status in Africa // Gusau International Journal of Management and Social Sciences, Federal University, Gusau. 2011.

104. Saliu H.A. Reflections on fifty years of Nigeria's foreign policy. In Segun Oshewolo. Major Contentions on Nigeria's Afrocentric Policy // India Quarterly: A Journal of International Affairs. 2019.

105. Sarpestein A. M. "The Enemy of My Enemy Is My Friend" Is the Enemy: Dealing with the War-Provoking Rules of Intent. Conflict Management and Peace Science. 2004.

106. Savicheva E.M. (eds). Features of the African vector of Muammar Gaddafi's foreign policy: from Arab unity to Pan-Africanism // Questions of History. Moscow. 2020. [In Russian]

107. Schlesinger Stephen. Can the United Nations Reform? // World Policy Journal. 1997.

108. Sinclair M. An Analysis of Nigerian Foreign Policy: The Evolution of Political Paranoia. Braamfontein: The South African Institute of International Relations, 1983.

109. Teryima Benjamin A. Continuities, and Discontinuities in Nigerian Foreign Policy // International Journal of Development and Sustainability. 2014.

110. Teryima Benjamin A. Concentricism in Nigeria's Foreign Policy // Journal of Humanities and Social Science. 2014.

111. Tony Monye. Nigeria-China Trade Relations: The Yawning Gaps, Zenith economic Quarterly. 2008.

112. Ujara Ese C. & Jide Ibietan. Foreign Policy in Nigeria's Fourth Republic: A Critical Analysis of Some Unresolved Issues // Journal of International and Global Studies. 2018.

113. Ujara Ese C. & Jide Ibietan. Citizen Diplomacy and Nigeria's International Image: The Social Constructivist Explanation // Covenant Journal of Business and Social Sciences. 2014.

114. Umezurike Samuel A. (Eds). Re-examining Nigeria's

Contributions to the African Union and the Domestic Socio-Economic Ramifications // Journal of Economics and Behavioral Studies. 2017.

115. Vladimir Shubin (Eds). Russia and Angola: the Rebirth of a Strategic Partnership? // Global Powers and Africa Programme, Occasional Paper № 154, 2013. [In Russian]

116. Vladimir Shubin. A united Africa? // Russian Council for International Affairs. 2014. [In Russian]

117. Walter Gam N. Cameroon. Too Much to Carry: The Perception and Ramifications of Boko Haram Activities on Cameroon // Conflict Studies Quarterly. 2013.

118. Warner J. (eds.). African Foreign Policies in International Institutions, Contemporary African Political Economy // Social Science Research Council. 2018.

119. William F.S. Miles. Development, Not Division Local Versus External Perceptions of the Niger-Nigeria Boundary // The Journal of Modern African Studies. 2005.

120. Wogu Ikedinachi A.P. (ed.). A Critical Evaluation of Nigeria's Foreign Policy at 53 // Research on Humanities and Social Sciences. 2015.

## Clerical documents

1. Abubakar Tafawa Balewa. Addis Ababa. 2009.

2. Abuja Agreement Resolution 1001, 1995.

3. Accra Summit to Review Regional Political, Security Situation. ECOWAS heads of state welcome the West African region's enormous progress. May 17, 2015.

4. African Union Report on UN Security Council Reform. Audit of the African Union Review High – Level Panel. 2005.

5. AU 50th Anniversary Solemn Declaration Adopted by the 21st Ordinary Session of the Assembly of Heads of State and Government of the African Union, at Addis Ababa held on 26 May 2013.

6. Colonial Office of Great Britain: Report of the Resumed Conference on the Nigerian Constitution Came.1959. London: HMSG 1954.

7. General Assembly Opens Debate on Group of Four Sponsored Draft Resolution on Security Council Reform. 2005.
8. General Assembly Resolutions. 1991 A (XVIII), UN GAOR, 18th Session. Supplement No. 15 Resolutions and Decisions, at 21, UN Doc. A/5515 (1963).
9. General Yakubu Gowon. Statement at the United Nations General Assembly // The New York Times Archives. 1973.
10. Manifesto of All Progressive Congress. All Rights Reserved. 2014.
11. New Partnership for Africa's Development. AU. 2001.
12. Nigeria and NEPAD. Facts: 1/1/1900.
13. Nigeria Structural Adjustment Program: Policies, Implementation, and Impact // The World Bank. 1994.
14. President Goodluck Jonathan. A Bad Account of an Equally Inglorious Era. // The Nations. November 26, 2018.
15. President Olusegun Obasanjo. The Presidential Legacy, 1999-2007 // Ibadan: Bookcraft. 2013.
16. President Umaru Musa Yar'Adua Seven-Point Agenda of the Federal Republic of Nigeria. Nigeria High Commission // Nigerian Ministry of Foreign Affairs, Abuja, Aso Rock. 2010.
17. Report of the UNGA transcript. The Chad Basin, Lifeline for People Nature and Peace. 2019.
18. Report of the ECOWAS Workshop. Lessons from ECOWAS. Peacekeeping Operations:1990 – 2004. Accra, 10-11 February 2005.
19. Report on the Mapping Sub-Saharan Africa's Future: Conference Summary. 2005.
20. Report of the Secretary-General. Security Council Fifty-second year. A/52/581, S/1997/866, 6 November 1997.
21. Special Motion of Thanks to the Leader of the Great Socialist Libya Arab Jamahiriya Brother Muammar Ghaddafi Adopted by the Fifth Extraordinary Session of the Assembly of Heads of State and Government. United Nations General Assembly. A/55/951. 2001.
22. The AU Agenda 2063.
23. The Berlin Conference of 1884/85.
24. The First Continental Report on the Implementation of Agenda 2063.

25. The House of Representatives Debates on Federation of Nigeria, August 20, 1960, cols 2669-71.
26. The UN 2015 Agenda for Millennium Development Goals.
27. The UN 2030 Agenda for Sustainable Development Goals.
28. The United Nations General Assembly Declaration on South Africa. 1989.
29. The UN 2015 Agenda for Millennium Development Goals. MDG Success Springboard for New Sustainable Development Agenda: UN Report. 2015.
30. The United Nations Security Council, Amendment 1963. Agenda 103(a).

## Mass Media

1. An interview with Olusegun Obasanjo: Up close and a little too personal // African Argument. September 28, 2017.
2. ECOWAS Chairman congratulates President Jonathan, General Buhari. Channels Television. 2015
3. EU-Nigeria trade volume hits N8.9trn // The Vanguard, October 5, 2018.
4. Inaugural Speech by President Goodluck Ebele Jonathan on 29 May 2011, Federal Ministry of Information, Abuja, Nigeria.
5. Inaugural Speech by President Muhammadu Buhari on 29 May 2015, Permanent Mission of Nigeria to the United Nations.
6. Inaugural Speech by President Olusegun Obasanjo, 29 May 1999, Federal Ministry of Information, Abuja.
7. Inaugural Speech by President Umaru Musa Yar'Adua. Nigerian Federal Ministry of Information & Communications, Vision 2020, Abuja, Aso Rock, 29 May 2007.
8. Lt. Gen. Olusegun Obasanjo. Nigeria First" in Call to Duty: A Collection of Speeches // Federal Ministry of Information, Lagos. 1978.
9. Nigerian foreign policy stays its Pan-Africanist course // Vanguard News, August 21, 2021.

10. Nigeria Interim Report. No. 24. February 29, 1984 // CSIS Africa Notes.

11. Nigeria in the World: Issues and Problems of the Sleeping Giant // This Day, 04 June 2001.

12. Olusegun Obasanjo. My Africa Utopia. AUDA – NEPAD //African Union Development Agency. 2015.

13. President Muhammadu Buhari. Approves NEPAD's Transformation into AU Development Agency // Premium Times, May 24, 2019.

14. President Muhammadu Buhari as the Chairman of Gulf of Guinea Commission // Independent, November 27, 2017.

15. President Muhammadu Buhari Calls for Reform of the African Union // Premium Times, February 7, 2021.

16. President Muhammadu Buhari Declaration on Lake Chad Region // Xinhua News Agency, May 25, 2021.

17. Report of President Olusegun Obasanjo Activities, Understanding Obasanjo's leadership and lesson // The Nations. January 20, 2013.

18. Restoring Peace in West Africa // Champion Newspapers Limited Lagos-Nigeria. 2010.

19. South Africa closes embassy in Nigeria // France, 5 Sep, 2019.

20. South Africa migrant attacks //Aljazeera, 4 Sep 2019.

21. Speech Delivered by Nelson Mandela at the United Nations. 2010.

22. Speech Delivered at the Maiden Interactive Session with the Diplomatic Corps Held at Rotunda Hall, Ministry of Foreign Affairs, Abuja on 12 December. 2015.

23. Speech Delivered by President Olusegun Obasanjo at Assembly of the Union Twenty-First Ordinary Session in Addis Ababa, Ethiopia. Assembly/AU/6(XXI) Original: English. SC10056. 2013.

24. Statement by Abubakar Tafawa Balewa. Prime Minister of the Federal Republic of Nigeria at the United Nations General Assembly, New York, October 7, 1960. Maiden General Assembly Statement at the United Nations.

25. Statement by Nnamdi Azikiwe. First President of Nigeria. The

Future of Pan-Africanism. Black Past. 2009.

26. The doctrine of Necessity // Sahara Reporter, Feb 13, 2010.

27. The History of Pan-Africanism. New Internationalist, 2000.

## Statistical sources

1. Nigeria Military Expenditure Database. SIPRI. 19 May 2008.

2. The World Bank. Country Data. IBRD – IDA. 19 May 2008.

3. Data on Nigeria of the African Continental Free Trade Area//Brookings. 22 September 2021.

4. Trade data sourced from the latest ONS publication of UK total trade. 2023.

5. Investment data sourced from the ONS ad-hoc

# Index

**A**

Addis Ababa, 49, 50, 51, 52, 57, 58, 148, 189, 192
African Continental Free Trade Agreement, viii, 64
African diplomacy, 11, 12, 76, 153
African Multilateral Affairs Department, 37
African Peer Review Mechanism, 56, 58
African Union, viii, 12, 14, 16, 33, 37, 38, 39, 49, 50, 53, 54, 55, 56, 57, 58, 59, 60, 63, 105, 106, 108, 134, 135, 147, 148, 151, 159, 160, 164, 181, 184, 185, 187, 188, 189, 191
Afrocentric foreign policy, 19, 20, 21, 22, 36, 43, 44, 77, 79, 80, 159
Afrocentrism, 11, 15, 27, 42, 43, 159, 180
Ahmed Salim, Salim, 101
Akinyemi, Bolaji, 34, 44, 108
Algeria-Nigeria Optic Fibre project, 60
Arthur Richards Constitution, 11, 15, 178
AU Agenda 2063, 57, 58, 59, 160, 190
AU Constitutive Act, 51
Azikiwe, Nnamdi, 47, 48

**B**

Babangida, Ibrahim, 23, 24, 63, 72, 74, 93, 94, 100, 101, 103, 104, 157, 162
Bakassi, 69, 149
Balewa, Tafawa, 17, 18, 19, 30, 32, 36, 42, 44, 61, 68, 87, 106, 151, 156, 166, 189, 192
Bande, Tijjani Muhammad, 150
Berlin Conference of 1884/85, 71, 190

Boko Haram, 28, 29, 85, 86, 90, 91, 92, 107, 110, 121, 130, 131, 133, 134, 135, 184, 188
Buhari, Muhammadu, 28, 29, 35, 53, 56, 58, 67, 68, 70, 72, 74, 75, 82, 83, 85, 86, 90, 91, 92, 93, 108, 128, 130, 134, 164, 185, 191, 192

**C**

Cameron, David, 32
China-Africa Cooperation Forum, 124
Chinese People's Liberation Army, 126
Cotonou Partnership Agreement, 14, 153, 154
Council of Legal Education, viii, 40
Council on Foreign Relations, 130

**D**

decolonisation of the continent., 12
Dogonyaro, Joshua, 80, 95, 96

**E**

East African Community, the Southern African Development Community, 37
Economic Community of West African States, viii, 16, 33, 38, 39, 45, 67, 74, 75, 76, 77, 78, 84, 87, 93, 94, 96, 100, 104, 159, 161, 162, 177, 179, 182, 183, 185
Eminent Persons Group, 111
European Union, viii, 14, 153, 154, 155, 165, 170, 180

**F**

Federal Ministry of Women Affairs and Social Development, viii, 40

Federation of International Football Association, viii, 41
First Nigeria-China Trade and Investment Forum, 125
Food and Agriculture Organisation, viii, 38
Forum for China-Africa Cooperation, 126

**G**

General Assembly of the United Nations, 16, 159
Germany, 14, 55, 74, 146, 165, 180
Ghaddafi, Muammar, 50, 51, 52, 53, 63, 190
Global Food Security Response System, 120
Gonsalves, Ralph, 143
Great Britain, 15, 19, 22, 23, 32, 66, 107, 108, 139, 145, 159, 189
Guinea-Bissau, 21, 22, 78, 158
Gulf of Guinea, viii, 13, 14, 37, 38, 39, 81, 83, 84, 85, 116, 127, 134, 162, 179, 191
Gulf of Guinea Commission, viii, 13, 14, 37, 38, 39, 81, 83, 84, 85, 162, 179, 191

**H**

Hugh Clifford Constitution, 11, 15, 179
Human Development Index, 120

**I**

International Civil Aviation Organisation, viii, 38
International Court of Justice, 69
International Labour Organisation, viii, 38
International Monetary Fund, viii, 38
Ironsi, Aguiyi, 106

**J**

Jonathan, Goodluck, 28, 79, 80, 90, 91, 107, 118, 181, 190, 191

**K**

Kagame, Paul, 53

**L**

Lake Chad Basin Commission, ix, 13, 14, 37, 38, 39, 81, 82, 83, 134, 162

**M**

Machiavelli, Niccolo, 11
Macpherson Constitution, 11, 15, 179
Mambilla hydro-electric project, 125
May, Theresa, 24, 25, 26, 29, 32, 42, 50, 56, 57, 74, 81, 83, 89, 90, 91, 92, 99, 102, 110, 111, 125, 131, 134, 160, 178, 179, 189, 191, 192
Mbeki, Thabo, 50
Middle East, 133
Millennium Declaration, 146
Ministry of Foreign Affairs, ix, 11, 17, 27, 29, 32, 33, 36, 37, 38, 43, 51, 52, 82, 83, 84, 85, 111, 126, 154, 155, 156, 159, 190, 192
Mozambique, 12, 20, 21, 22, 62, 107, 150, 151
Muhammed, Murtala, 22
Multinational Joint Task Force, 134, 135
Museveni, Yoweri, 51, 101

**N**

Namibia, 12, 20, 22, 62, 107, 150, 151, 152
National Agency for the Prohibition of Trafficking in Persons, ix, 40
National Boundary Commission, ix, 72, 73, 74, 161
National Union for the Total Independence of Angola, 22, 107

New Partnership for Africa's Development, ix, 12, 54, 56, 58, 160, 189
Niger Delta, 90, 118, 125, 157
Nigeria–Biafra civil war, 22, 75
Nigerian Investment Promotion Commission, 125
Nigerian Law ReformCommission, 40
Nigerian National Petroleum Corporation, ix, 41, 128
Nigeria-UK bilateral relations, 13, 109, 162
Nollywood, 21, 184
Non-Aligned Movement, 16, 33, 159
Nwachukwu, Aja, 16, 23

**O**

Obasanjo, Olusegun, 22, 24, 25, 26, 27, 41, 49, 50, 51, 52, 55, 63, 79, 80, 83, 89, 90, 107, 109, 110, 149, 152, 157, 158, 184, 186, 187, 190, 191, 192
Oliver Lyttleton Constitution, 11, 15, 179
Onyeama, Geoffrey, 131
Onyia, Dubem, 122
Organisation of African Unity, ix, 12, 49, 50, 53, 54, 63, 101, 105, 106, 151, 160
Organisation of Petroleum Exporting Countries, 37

**P**

Pan-African Movement, 47, 159
Pan-Africanism, 12, 20, 47, 48, 59, 87, 159, 184, 188, 192
Pax Nigeriana, 108
Petroleum Technology Development Fund, ix, 41
Popular Movement for the Liberation of Angola, 22, 107
Presidential Advisory Council on International Relations, ix, 11, 36, 41

**Q**

Queen Elizabeth II, 15

**R**

Regional Centre for Maritime Security of West Africa, viii, 84
Regional Maritime Security of Central Africa, viii, 84
Russia, viii, 13, 55, 107, 127, 128, 129, 130, 131, 164, 183, 185, 188
Russia-Africa Summit in Sochi, 14, 129, 164

**S**

Sao Tome and Principe, 21, 158
Saudi Arabia, 26
Shagari, Shehu, 19, 22, 23
Shinkaiye, Kayode, 51
Sino-African Cooperation, 124
South Africa, viii, 12, 20, 21, 22, 31, 42, 46, 50, 51, 52, 53, 54, 56, 62, 63, 107, 137, 139, 147, 148, 149, 150, 151, 165, 182, 186, 190, 192
Stallard, Peter, 17
Structural Adjustment Programme, 23, 63

**T**

Taylor, Charles, 100, 103
Trans-Sahel Counter-Terrorism Programme, 121

**U**

Union of Soviet Socialist Republics, 13, 22, 107, 127, 164
United Nations Educational Scientific and Cultural Organisat-ion, 39
United Nations General Assembly, ix, 17, 20, 42, 44, 53, 61, 82, 87, 106, 150, 151, 189, 190, 192

United Nations Operation in the Congo, 106
United Nations Security Council, 137, 138, 140, 144, 164, 185, 190

**W**

Wade, Abdoulaye, 51
World Bank, 24, 38, 63, 99, 189, 192

**X**

Xiaojie, Gu, 125

**Y**

Yar'Adua, Musa, 19, 27, 28, 90, 118, 179, 190, 191

www.ingramcontent.com/pod-product-compliance
Lightning Source LLC
Chambersburg PA
CBHW041130280326
41928CB00059B/3330